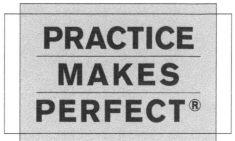

PRACTICE
MAKES
PERFECT®

Arabic Pronouns and Prepositions

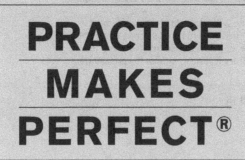

Arabic
Pronouns and
Prepositions

Otared Haidar, PhD

New York   Chicago   San Francisco   Lisbon   London   Madrid   Mexico City
Milan   New Delhi   San Juan   Seoul   Singapore   Sydney   Toronto

8 9 10 11 12 13   QVS/QVS   22 21 20 19 18

ISBN   978-0-07-175973-1
MHID   0-07-175973-5

e-ISBN   978-0-07-175974-8
e-MHID   0-07-175974-3

Library of Congress Control Number 2012931083

Interior design by Village Bookworks, Inc.

McGraw-Hill products are available at special quantity discounts to use as premiums
and sales promotions or for use in corporate training programs. To contact a
representative, please e-mail us at bulksales@mcgraw-hill.com.

This book is printed on acid-free paper.

Contents

Preface

Pronouns and prepositions are two essential parts of speech. Learning the grammatical rules of pronouns and prepositions is a preliminary task for anyone who is studying Arabic. Practicing them to consolidate learning their types and functions is a task that continues for many subsequent stages.

Most teachers and students of languages agree on considering pronouns as an area that will take lots of effort from both sides to master. In addition, the system of Arabic pronouns has its own distinctiveness such as having the dual system and the attachable pronouns. As for prepositions, my undergraduate students who are studying for a BA in Arabic and European Languages at Oxford University insist that prepositions are a tricky area to master in any new language and sometimes difficult to translate. This particularity of pronouns and prepositions is also viewed as a challenge by my graduate students studying at a more advanced level. Therefore, mastering pronouns and prepositions and acquiring the sufficient knowledge about their rules depend mainly on practicing them and these exactly are the main goals that this book aspires to achieve.

To give a thorough understanding of the subject and to allow the reader to acquire sufficient knowledge on this important area of Arabic grammar, the definition of "pronoun" and "preposition" draws on both their definitions in Arabic and English.

Practice Makes Perfect: Arabic Pronouns and Prepositions covers all the areas that are related to the Arabic pronouns and prepositions. It has sufficient illustrative examples for all types of these two parts of speech and their forms and functions. In addition, it makes the learning process more productive and interesting by basing the learning on providing numerous exercises and texts to practice. The book is suitable for students in self-study courses as well as for students and teachers in courses and programs.

PRONOUNS

Pronouns constitute an essential part of speech that can substitute for a noun or a nominal phrase. Pronouns are categorized according to their functions in the sentences: subject pronouns, possessive pronouns, object pronouns, prepositional pronouns, relative pronouns, and interrogative pronouns.

In addition to being categorized according to their functions, Arabic pronouns are also classified according to their form into two types: separate pronouns and attached pronouns.

Subject pronouns

Introduction to subject pronouns

Subject pronouns are also called personal pronouns. The twelve subject pronouns are separate pronouns and they stand alone. The second and third subject pronouns include pronouns for dual, masculine, and feminine, as well as pronouns for plural feminine. There is no equivalent for "it" in Arabic.

The subject pronouns are:

PLURAL		DUAL		SINGULAR	
we	نحن			I	أنا
you (pl. m.)	أنتم	you (d. m. f.)	أنتما	you (s. m.)	أنتَ
you (pl. f.)	أنتن			you (s. f.)	أنتِ
they (pl. m.)	هم	they (d. m. f.)	هما	he	هو
they (pl. f.)	هن			she	هي

Gender

Note that:

1. Masculine predominates when it refers to a mixed group. Compare the following:

   John, Mary, and Layla are students in the department of Arabic Studies and they are my students.   جون وماري وليلى طلاب في قسم اللغة العربية وهم طلابي.

   Nola, Mary, and Layla are students in the department of Arabic Studies and they are my students.   نولا وماري وليلى طالبات في قسم اللغة العربية وهن طالباتي.

2. There is no gender specification for the first person.

   I am a student.   أنا طالب.

   I am a student.   أنا طالبة.

   We are students.   نحن طلاب.

   We are students.   نحن طالبات.

3. There are no special duals for the first person.

I am with John in the café and we are having coffee.	أنا مع جون في المقهى ونحن نتناول القهوة.

Duals for second person and third person have one form each, for both genders.

They are two (m.) old friends.	هما صديقان قديمان.
They are two (f.) old friends.	هما صديقتان قديمتان.
You are two (m.) smart students.	أنتما طالبان ذكيان.
You are two (f.) smart students.	أنتما طالبتان ذكيتان.

4. There is no equivalent for the pronoun "it." Thus, nonhuman nouns are referred to by "he" or "she" according to their genders.

I live in the city of Alexandria and it is a beautiful city.	أسكن في مدينة الاسكندرية وهي مدينة جميلة.
The restaurant is in the town center and it is a small restaurant.	المطعم في وسط المدينة وهو مطعم صغير.

Nonhuman plural takes the subject pronoun of a third person feminine singular.

We visited the markets in the old city of Damascus and they are famous markets.	زرنا الأسواق في مدينة دمشق القديمة وهي أسواق شهيرة.
We saw Oxford's colleges and they are ancient colleges.	رأينا كليات أكسفورد وهي كليات عريقة.

Second person formal pronouns

The pronoun "أنتم", which refers to the second person masculine plural, can be used in a very formal situation to address a singular high-profile masculine or feminine personality. This alteration of the pronoun affects the other elements of the sentence.

Please tell the minister, "You are invited to the meeting."	من فضلك قل للوزيرة، "أنتم مدعوون للاجتماع."
You are right, Sir! And I totally agree with you.	أنتم على حق يا سيدِي، وأنا أتفق معكم تماماً.

Arabic nominal sentences

An Arabic nominal sentence consists of a subject and predicate and its subject can be a pronoun. Unlike the Arabic verbal sentence, the Arabic nominal sentence always takes the same order of the nominal sentence in English. Similarly, the subject pronoun is usually the first element in the sentence. However, unlike the English nominal sentence, an Arabic nominal sentence does not take the verb "to be" when the sentence is in the present tense.

He is a teacher.	هو أستاذ.
You are teachers.	أنتم أساتذة.

The following sentences are about citizens of different Arab countries and their nationalities. Translate the following sentences into English, and define the gender and number (singular, dual, or plural) of each nationality holder.

EXAMPLES   *I am Lebanese (s. m.).* أنا لبناني

                They are Somalians (pl. f.). هن صوماليات

١ أنا جزائري. _____

٢ أنا عراقية. _____

٣ نحن سوريون. _____

٤ نحن مصريات. _____

٥ أنتَ مغربي. _____

٦ أنتِ إماراتية. _____

٧ أنتما سعوديان. _____

٨ أنتما يمنيتان. _____

٩ أنتم تونسيون. _____

١٠ أنتن أردنيات. _____

١١ هو بحريني. _____

١٢ هي قطرية. _____

١٣ هما سودانيان. _____

١٤ هما فلسطينيتان. _____

١٥ هم ليبيون. _____

١٦ هن كويتيات. _____

Write the appropriate subject pronouns for the following nouns.

EXAMPLE   __ هو أستاذ__ He is a teacher. أستاذ.

١ _____ طالب. I am a student (s. m.).

٢ _____ دكتورة. I am a doctor (s. f.).

٣ _____ مهندسون. We are engineers (pl. m.).

٤ _____ ممرضات. We are nurses (pl. f.).

You are a friend (s. m.). صديق ‎_____ ٥

You are a colleague (s. f.). زميلة ‎_____ ٦

You are Egyptians (d. m.). مصريان ‎_____ ٧

You are Moroccan (d. f.). مغربيتان ‎_____ ٨

You are in the classroom (pl. m.). في الصف ‎_____ ٩

You are teachers (pl. f.). مدرسات ‎_____ ١٠

He is Syrian (s. m.). سوري ‎_____ ١١

She is Jordanian (s. f.). أردنية ‎_____ ١٢

They are Lebanese (d. m.). لبنانيان ‎_____ ١٣

They are employees (d. f.). موظفتان ‎_____ ١٤

They are in the library (pl. m.). في المكتبة ‎_____ ١٥

They are in the garden (pl. f.). في الحديقة ‎_____ ١٦

EXERCISE
1·3

Emphasize the sentences by deriving the appropriate subject pronoun from these verbal sentences.

EXAMPLES   أدرس العربية. أنا أدرس العربية. ‎_____

ندرس العربية. نحن ندرس العربية. ‎_____

يدرس العربية. هو يدرس العربية. ‎_____

أكتب رسالة. ‎_____ ١

نحب مشاهدة الأفلام القديمة. ‎_____ ٢

تكتب وظيفتكَ. ‎_____ ٣

تقرأين الدرس. ‎_____ ٤

تزوران أصدقاءكما. ‎_____ ٥

تعرفون عدة لغات. ‎_____ ٦

تستمعن إلى الموسيقى. ‎_____ ٧

يسكنون في هذا البيت. ‎_____ ٨

يشتري الجريدة. ‎_____ ٩

تتذكر أصدقاء طفولتها. ‎_____ ١٠

١١ ــــــــــــــــــــــــــــ يحبان أختهما الصغيرة.

١٢ ــــــــــــــــــــــــــــ تحترمان والديهما.

١٣ ــــــــــــــــــــــــــــ يجلسون في المقهى.

١٤ ــــــــــــــــــــــــــــ يسهرن في النادي.

١٥ ــــــــــــــــــــــــــــ ستفتتحون الاجتماع يا سيادة الرئيس.

◆ EXERCISE
1·4

Translate the following sentences into Arabic.

EXAMPLE   He is at home. هو في البيت.

١ We are friends. ــ

٢ She is a student. ــ

٣ You are a father. ــ

٤ You are a mother. ــ

٥ You are parents. ــ

٦ You are two girls. ــ

٧ You are brothers (pl. m.). ــ

٨ You are sisters (pl. f.). ــ

٩ I am here. ــ

١٠ He is there. ــ

١١ They are two men. ــ

١٢ They are two women. ــ

١٣ They are paternal uncles (pl. m.). ــ

١٤ They are maternal aunts (pl. f.). ــ

Subject markers

The verb form in Arabic, both past and present, includes a subject marker. The subject marker indicates the person, gender, and number. Hence, the pronoun adds more emphasis to the verbal sentence. Nonetheless, Arabic verbal sentences can stand without a pronoun.

EXERCISE
1·5

The following sentences include verbs in parentheses that indicate the third person singular "he." Conjugate these verbs to adjust them to the accompanying pronouns and then drop the pronouns. Translate the adjusted sentences into English.

EXAMPLE

نحن (يتناول) القهوة معاً كل صباح. <u>نتناول القهوة معاً كل صباح.</u>

<u>*We drink coffee together every morning.*</u>

١ هي (يستمع) إلى الموسيقى العربية. _____

_____

٢ أنتماأخوان وأنتما (يسكن) في بيت كبير. _____

_____

٣ نحن (يعمل) في مصنع السيارات. _____

_____

٤ هو (يشاهد) المباريات الرياضية على التلفاز _____

_____

٥ هل أنت الطالب الجديد؟ وهل أنتَ (يدرس) العربية؟ _____

_____

٦ هما صديقتان قديمتان وهما (يزور) بيتنا كل أسبوع. _____

_____

٧ أنتِ (يطبخ) لزوجكِ وأولادكِ يوم الجمعة. _____

_____

٨ هن (يساعد) والدتهن في عمل البيت. _____

_____

٩ أنتن (يعتني) بأولادكن كثيراً. _____

_____

١٠ هما طالبان في السنة الثالثة وهما سوف (يتخرج) السنة القادمة. _____

_____

١١ أنتم (يحب) مساعدة كل جيرانكم. _____

_____

١٢ أنا (يحب) قراءة الروايات العاطفية. _____

_____

١٣ هم (يكتب) رسائل إلى أصدقائهم في عيد الميلاد. _____

_____

١٤ أنتما زميلان وأنتما (يعمل) في نفس الشركة. _____

_____

The subject pronoun "it"

The two pronouns for masculine third person singular and feminine third person singular stand for masculine and feminine "it," respectively. As for nonhuman masculine and feminine plurals, they take the feminine third person singular.

It is a beautiful house in London.	هو بيت جميل في لندن.
It is a nice cat.	هي قطة لطيفة.
They are nice houses.	هي بيوت جميلة.

EXERCISE

1·6

Rewrite the sentences by replacing the words or phrases in boldface with the appropriate subject pronouns. Translate the new sentences into English.

EXAMPLE   القلم على الطاولة. هو على الطاولة.

It is on the table.

١ **كلب صديقي** كلب ضخم وجميل. _____

_____

٢ **فكرة** عظيمة مثل كل أفكاره. _____

_____

٣ أكلت **القطة** اللحم. _____

_____

٤ **الكلاب** في الشوارع. _____

_____

٥ القطط في البيوت. _____

_____

٦ الكتاب القديم على الطاولة الجديدة. _____

_____

٧ الجريدة على الكرسي. _____

_____

٨ الكتب في المكتبة. _____

_____

٩ البيت قريب من النهر. _____

_____

١٠ المقهى بعيد عن الجامعة. _____

_____

١١ سيارة المدير جميلة وجديدة. _____

_____

١٢ نامت القطة على الأريكة. _____

_____

١٣ الكلب يحب الأولاد. _____

_____

١٤ قصص الحب ممتعة وأنا أحب قراءتها في العطلة. _____

_____

١٥ المقاهي العربية في لندن جميلة وأنا أحب الجلوس فيها. _____

_____

Possessive pronouns ·2·

Introduction to possessive pronouns

Possessive pronouns are attached pronouns and they indicate affiliation and belonging. This group of pronouns is part of the Arabic attached pronouns that can be attached like suffixes to singular, dual, and plural nouns.

PLURAL		DUAL		SINGULAR	
our	نا...			my	ي...
your (pl. m.)	كم...	your (d. m. f.)	كما...	your (s. m.)	كَ...
your (pl. f.)	كن...			your (s. f.)	كِ...
their (pl. m.)	هم...	their (d. m. f.)	هما...	his	ه...
their (pl. f.)	هن...			her	ها...

The personal pronoun kum

Note that the pronoun **kum**, which refers to the second person masculine plural, can be used in a very formal situation to address a singular high-profile masculine or feminine personality. This use of the pronoun affects the other elements of the sentence, and they should be put in plural.

father	والد
my father	والدي
our father	والدنا
your father (s. m.)	والدكَ
your father (s. f.)	والدكِ
your father (d. m.)	والدكما
your father (d. f.)	والدكما
your father (pl. m.)	والدكم
your father (pl. f.)	والدكن
his father	والده
her father	والدها

their father (d. m.)	والدهما
their father (d. f.)	والدهما
their father (pl. m.)	والدهم
their father (pl. f.)	والدهن

The **ta' marbuta**

The **ta' marbuta**, which occurs at the end of the feminine nouns and adjectives, will be rendered into a letter "ت" when it is attached to a pronoun.

mother	والدة
my mother	والدتي
our mother	والدتنا
your mother (s. m.)	والدتكَ
your mother (s. f.)	والدتكِ
your mother (d. m.)	والدتكما
your mother (d. f.)	والدتكما
your mother (pl. m.)	والدتكم
your mother (pl. f.)	والدتكن
his mother	والدته
her mother	والدتها
their mother (d. m.)	والدتهما
their mother (d. f.)	والدتهما
their mother (pl. m.)	والدتهم
their mother (pl. f.)	والدتهن

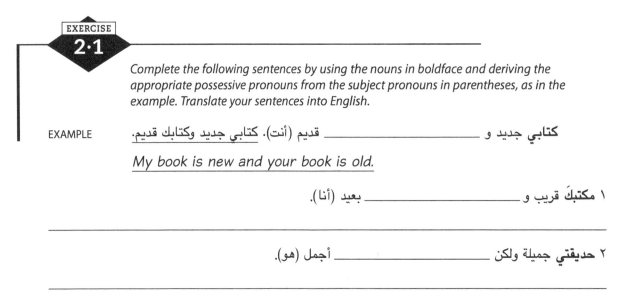

EXERCISE
2·1

Complete the following sentences by using the nouns in boldface and deriving the appropriate possessive pronouns from the subject pronouns in parentheses, as in the example. Translate your sentences into English.

EXAMPLE   كتابي جديد و ــــــــــــــــــــــــ قديم (أنت). <u>كتابي جديد وكتابك قديم.</u>
<u>My book is new and your book is old.</u>

١ مكتبكَ قريب و ـــــــــــــــــــــــ بعيد (أنا).

_____

٢ حديقتي جميلة ولكن ـــــــــــــــــــــ أجمل (هو).

_____

٣ بابنا من الخشب و _____ من الحديد (أنتم).

_____

٤ زوجكِ مهندس و _____ طبيب (هي).

_____

٥ والدتهن في العمل و _____ في البيت (أنتن).

_____

٦ بيتكم في المدينة و _____ في الريف (هم).

_____

٧ أولادهما في البيت و _____ في الملعب (أنتما).

_____

٨ سيارتكم حمراء و _____ زرقاء (نحن).

_____

٩ أسرتها صغيرة و _____ كبيرة (أنتِ).

_____

١٠ عملكم سهل و _____ صعب (هن).

_____

١١ غرفتكما صغيرة و _____ واسعة (هما).

_____

١٢ مدرستها في شمال المدينة و _____ في الجنوب (أنتِ).

_____

EXERCISE

2·2

Rewrite each phrase replacing the word in boldface with a possessive pronoun.
Translate the new phrases into English.

EXAMPLE   أضواء المدينة أضواؤها

Its lights

١ كتاب الأستاذ _____

_____

٢ مكتب المديرة _____

_____

٣ بيت أصدقائي _____

_____

٤ لون الوردة _____ _____

_____

٥ احترام الوالدين _____ _____

_____

٦ مكتبة الجامعة _____ _____

_____

٧ ألعاب أولاده _____ _____

_____

٨ بيت خالي _____ _____

_____

٩ قلم الطالبة _____ _____

_____

١٠ زوجة عمكم _____ _____

_____

١١ سيارة المهندس _____ _____

_____

١٢ طاولة السكرتيرة _____ _____

_____

١٣ باب بيتنا _____ _____

_____

١٤ أصوات السيارات _____ _____

_____

١٥ صور صديقاتهن _____ _____

_____

١٦ لون العينين _____ _____

_____

١٧ حديقة جيرانه _____ _____

_____

١٨ ذكريات طفولتك _____ _____

_____

١٩ أسماء بناته _____ _____

_____

٢٠ غرفة الطفلين _____ _____

_____

Rewrite the following phrases by changing the subject pronouns into possessive pronouns, as in the example. Translate the new phrases into English.

EXAMPLE   قلم (هو) قلمه

His pen

١ كتاب (أنا) _____

_____

٢ بيت (نحن) _____

_____

٣ دراجة (أنتَ) _____

_____

٤ عائلة (أنتِ) _____

_____

٥ صديق (أنتما) (d. m.) _____

_____

٦ جار (أنتما) (d. f.) _____

_____

٧ مدرسة (أنتم) _____

_____

٨ مدينة (أنتن) _____

_____

٩ طفل (هو) _____

_____

١٠ أستاذ (هي) _____

_____

١١ جامعة (هما) (d. m.) _____

_____

١٢ سيارة (هما) (d. f.) _____

_____

١٣ حديقة (هم) _____

_____

١٤ أخت (هن) _____

_____

١٥ جلالة (أنتم) _____

_____

Translate these sentences into English.

EXAMPLE   غرفتنا كبيرة. *Our room is big.*

١ أنا أحب عائلتي. _____

٢ بيتنا قرب النهر. _____

٣ صديقك جورج لطيف. _____

٤ كتابك جديد ياعزيزتي سميرة. _____

٥ قلت لسعيد وسعاد، "والدتكما ذكية جداً." _____

٦ قلنا لها ومنى، "والدكما غني." _____

٧ أستاذكم في المكتب. _____

٨ جامعتكن شهيرة. _____

٩ سيارته قديمة. _____

١٠ دراجتها جديدة. _____

١١ لي صديقان هما فؤاد وخالد، وأختهما اسمها ليلى. _____

١٢ صديقتاي اسمهما هناء وسناء، وأخوهما اسمه سمير. _____

١٣ جارهم لطيف. _____

١٤ مدرستهن قريبة من بيتهن. _____

١٥ أريد مقابلة جلالتكم. _____

The **idafa** construction

The first word of **idafa** construction never takes a pronoun. The pronoun is to be attached to the second word of **idafa**. Look at the following example where the first word of **idafa** is underlined.

my travel ticket	تذكرة سفري
our sitting room	غرفة جلوسنا
your toothache	ألم أسنانك
their swimming suits	ثياب سباحتهم
his identity card	بطاقة هويته

Rewrite each phrase, replacing the subject pronoun in parentheses with a possessive pronoun. Translate your phrases into English.

EXAMPLE   اسم زميل (أنا) <u>اسم زميلي</u>

The name of my colleague

١ ساعة يد(أنا) _____

_____

٢ شباك غرفة (نحن) _____

_____

٣ عنوان بيت (أنتَ) _____

_____

٤ غطاء طاولة (أنتِ) _____

_____

٥ إبريق شاي (أنتما) _____

_____

٦ صديقة طفولة(أنتما) _____

_____

٧ فناجين قهوة (أنتم) _____

_____

٨ علبة بريد (هن) _____

_____

٩ باب مكتب (هو) _____

_____

١٠ غطاء رأس (هي) _____

_____

١١ غرفة نوم (هما) _____

_____

١٢ طاولة مطبخ (هما) _____

_____

١٣ أغطية سرير(هو) _____

_____

١٤ رقم هاتف (أنتن) _____

_____

Adjectives in the **idafa** construction

Adjectives cannot come between the modifying noun and its attached suffix. The following example shows the wrong use of the adjective.

أخت الجميلة ه

The correct use is as follows:

أخته الجميلة   his pretty sister

If the adjective modifies a noun with a possessive pronoun, then it follows the noun and its attached pronoun. The possessive pronoun turns a noun into a definite noun. Hence, the adjective agrees with the noun and takes a definite article as well. "The" is the definite article. The adjectives are in boldface in the following examples.

أخته **الجميلة**   his pretty sister

بيتنا **القديم**   our old house

EXERCISE
2·6

Translate these sentences into English.

EXAMPLE   شقتنا الصغيرة   *Our small flat*

١ طالباتي المتفوقات

٢ خالاتنا وعماتنا العزيزات

٣ جدتك المحبة

٤ عمك المفضل

٥ طفلكما الصغير

٦ حديقتكما الجميلة

٧ أختكم الكبرى

٨ مدرستكن الابتدائية

٩ ابنه الصغير

١٠ طلابها الجدد

١١ ابنتهما الوحيدة

١٢ صديقتهما القديمة

١٣ عنوانهم القديم

١٤ والدتهن اللطيفة

The idafa with multiple nouns

If the **idafa** refers to two nouns or more then it must follow the first one, and the relevant referent suffix (possessive pronoun) should refer to the **idafa** (the second word in the construction) and be attached to the rest of the nouns.

The teacher's house and car	بيت الأستاذ وسيارته
The students' books, notebooks, pens, papers, and bags are on the table.	كتب الطلاب ودفاترهـم وأقلامـهم وحقائبهم على الطاولة.

EXERCISE

2·7

Translate the following sentences into English.

EXAMPLE   *The student's pen and paper* قلم الطالب وورقته

١ طاولة المدير وكرسيه _____

٢ بيت الجار وحديقته _____

٣ والد الطفل ووالدته _____

٤ زوجة جارنا وابنته _____

٥ بداية السنة ونهايتها _____

٦ رأس القطة وذيلها _____

٧ مساعد المدير وسكرتيرته _____

٨ كتب الطلاب ودفاترهم _____

٩ باب الغرفة وشباكها _____

١٠ روايات الكاتب وقصصه القصيرة _____

The singular nouns *father* and *brother*

The two singular nouns أخ and أب (*father* and *brother*, respectively) can stand alone and behave like typical Arabic nouns. However, they are part of a group called the *Six Nouns* that show case endings as long vowels when they have possessive pronouns (or an **idafa**), except with the first person singular. Look at the following examples and notice how the short vowel **damma**, **fatha**, or **kasra** turns into the equivalent long vowel when the noun is followed by a possessive pronoun.

Nominative: أبوك، أخوك

Your father came.	جاء أبوك.

Accusative: أباك، أخاك

I know your father.	أعرف أبـاك.

Genitive: أبيك، أخيك

I asked about your father.	سألت عن أبيك.

Nominative, accusative, and genitive: أبي، أخي

EXERCISE
2·8

Complete the following sentences by combining the subject pronouns and possessive pronouns.

EXAMPLE هذا هو _____ (أخ، هي). <u>هذا هو أخوها.</u>

Nominative:

١ جاء _____ وأمه إلى اجتماع الآباء في مدرستنا (أب، هو).

٢ أنت صديقي ومثل _____ (أخ، أنا).

٣ هل زاركم _____ (أخ، أنتم)؟

٤ _____ يحبنا كثيراً (أب، نحن).

٥ _____ صديقي (أخ، أنت).

٦ قرأ _____ الجريدة (أب، هي).

٧ أين _____ (أب، أنت)؟

٨ كتب _____ الرسالة (أخ، هن).

٩ _____ أستاذ في الجامعة (أب، أنتما).

١٠ أمهم في البيت و_____ في العمل (أب، هم).

١١ _____ طالب في الجامعة (أخ، أنتن).

١٢ _____ رجل طيب (أب، هما).

١٣ حدثنا _____ عن رحلته إلى بغداد (أخ، أنتما).

Accusative:

١٤ قابلت _____ أمس (أخ، أنت).

١٥ أعطت _____ الكتاب (أخ، هي).

١٦ أحب _____ كثيراً (أب، أنا).

١٧ أعرف أمه و_____ (أب، هو).

١٨ هل أخبرتم _____ (أخ، أنتم)؟

١٩ نحترم _____ كثيراً (أب، نحن).

٢٠ شاهدنا _____ في الحفلة (أخ، هم).

٢١ زرت _____ في مكتبه (أخ، أنت).

٢٢ يساعدن _____ في العناية بالحديقة (أب، هن).

٢٣ انتظرنا _____ في المحطة (أب، أنتن).

٢٤ أنا درَّستُ _____ في الجامعة (أخ، هما).

20 PRONOUNS

٢٥ ستسافر مع _____ (أخ، هي).

٢٦ جاء مع _____ وأمه إلى الحفلة (أب، هو).

٢٧ صديقي يسكن مع _____ (أخ، أنت).

٢٨ سافر مع _____ و _____ (أب، أخ، أنا).

٢٩ سيتكلم المدير مع _____ (أب، أنتم).

٣٠ قدمن الهدية إلى _____ في عيد ميلاده (أخ، نحن).

٣١ ستقضي العيد مع أمها و _____ (أب، هي).

٣٢ استمعنا إلى _____ وهو يغني في الحفلة (أخ، أنت).

٣٣ اتصلن بـ _____ عند وصولهن (أب، هن).

٣٤ تعرفت على _____ منذ سنة (أب، أنتما).

٣٥ أخي يلعب كرة القدم مع _____ (أخ، هم).

٣٦ أخي يدرس مع _____ (أخ، أنتن).

٣٧ هذا الموظف يعمل في مكتب _____ (أب، هما).

Dropping the nūn in idafa

The **nūn** ن in the dual case endings "ان، ين" and in the sound masculine plural endings "ون، ين" is dropped whenever the noun takes a possessive pronoun or an **idafa**. Note that with the first person singular, the two ي will be joined in one ي with a **shadda** يّ. The letter that precedes the ي takes a **fatha** in the dual form, and a **kasra** in the sound plural.

Dual form in nominative: صديقاه، صديقاي

His two friends have come.   جاء صديقاه.

Dual form in accusative and genitive: صديقَيه، صديقَيّ

I know his two friends.   أعرف صديقيه.

I asked about his two friends.   سألت عن صديقيه.

Sound masculine plural in nominative: مدرسوه، مدرسِيّ

Sound masculine plural in accusative and genitive: مدرسيه، مدرسِيّ

Combine these nouns with their pronouns.

EXAMPLE   صديقان (نحن) <u>صديقانا</u>

Nominative:

١ معلمون (أنت) _____

٢ طفلان (هما) _____

٣ مساعدون (نحن) _____

٤ والدان (أنتم) _____

٥ مدربون (هن) _____

٦ زميلتان (أنت) _____

٧ زائران (أنتن) _____

٨ مشاهدون (هي) _____

٩ جاران (أنتما) _____

١٠ قائلون (هو) _____

١١ سكرتيرتان (هم) _____

١٢ نائبان (أنا) _____

Accusative and genitive:

١٣ معلمَين (أنت) _____

١٤ طفلين (هما) _____

١٥ مساعدَين (نحن) _____

١٦ والدَين (أنتم) _____

١٧ مدربَين (هن) _____

١٨ زميلتين (أنت) _____

١٩ زائرَين (أنتن) _____

٢٠ مشاهدَين (هي) _____

٢١ جارين (أنتم) _____

٢٢ قائلَين (هو) _____

٢٣ سكرتيرتين (هم) _____

٢٤ نائبين (أنا) _____

The possessive pronoun "it"

There is no equivalent for the possessive pronoun "it." Thus, nonhuman nouns are referred to by "his" or "her" according to their genders. Both masculine and feminine nonhuman plurals take the possessive pronoun of a third person feminine singular.

EXERCISE
2·10

Rewrite each sentence, replacing the words in boldface with the appropriate possessive pronouns as in the example. Translate the new phrases into English.

EXAMPLE   الجامعة وطلابها الجامعة وطلاب الجامعة

The university and its students

١ الشركة ومدير الشركة _____

_____

٢ كتاب اللغة العربية الجديد وصفحات كتاب **اللغة العربية الجديد** _____

_____

٣ مكتبات الجامعة وكتب مكتبات الجامعة _____

_____

٤ البيوت وأبواب البيوت _____

_____

٥ الموسيقى الكلاسيكية ونغمات الموسيقى الكلاسيكية _____

_____

٦ النوافذ وستائر النوافذ _____

_____

٧ الجامعة القديمة وطلاب الجامعة القديمة _____

_____

٨ الغرفة وأثاث الغرفة _____ .

_____

٩ المكاتب و موظفو المكاتب _____

_____

١٠ القلم وحبر القلم _____

_____

١١ البحر وأمواج البحر _____

_____

١٢ الأقفال ومفاتيح **الأقفال** _____

_____

١٣ طاولة العشاء الجديدة وغطاء **الطاولة** الملون الجديد _____

_____

١٤ المدرسة الابتدائية وأساتذة **المدرسة الابتدائية** المتخصصون في اللغة العربية _____

_____

١٥ القمر وضوء **القمر** _____

_____

١٦ الشمس وأشعة **الشمس** _____

_____

١٧ النجوم وأنوار **النجوم** _____

_____

١٨ المدن الكبيرة وسكان **المدن الكبيرة** المشغولون بالعمل دائماً _____

_____

١٩ الفصول وتنوع **الفصول** _____

_____

٢٠ الربيع وجمال **الربيع** _____

_____

٢١ الشتاء ومطر **الشتاء** _____

_____

٢٢ القهوة العربية بالهال ونكهة **القهوة العربية بالهال** _____

_____

٢٣ الأنهار وضفاف **الأنهار** _____

_____

٢٤ الورود الدمشقية العطرة و ألوان **الورود الدمشقية العطرة** _____

_____

٢٥ شجرة الياسمين وعطر **شجرة الياسمين** _____

_____

Object pronouns

Introduction to object pronouns

Object pronouns are also attached pronouns that can be attached as suffixes to past and present-tense verbs to substitute a direct object.

PLURAL		DUAL		SINGULAR	
us	...نا			me	...ني
you (pl. m.)	...كم	you (d. m. f.)	...كما	you (s. m.)	...كَ
you (pl. f.)	...كن			you (s. f.)	...كِ
them (pl. m.)	...هم	them (d. m. f.)	...هما	him	...ه
them (pl. f.)	...هن			her	...ها

The personal pronoun kum

The pronoun **kum**, which refers to the second person masculine plural, can be used in a very formal situation to address a singular high-profile masculine or feminine personality. This alteration of the pronoun affects the other elements of the sentence.

He knows me.	هو يعرفني.
He knows us.	هو يعرفنا.
He knows you (s. m.).	هو يعرفكَ.
He knows you (s. f.).	هو يعرفكِ.
He knows you (d. m.).	هو يعرفكما.
He knows you (d. f.).	هو يعرفكما.
He knows you (pl. m.).	هو يعرفكم.
He knows you (pl. f.).	هو يعرفكن.
He knows him.	هو يعرفه.
He knows her.	هو يعرفها.
He knows them (d. m.).	هو يعرفهما.
He knows them (d. f.).	هو يعرفهما.
He knows them (pl. m.).	هو يعرفهم.
He knows them (pl. f.).	هو يعرفهن.

EXERCISE

3·1

Complete the following sentences as shown in the example and translate them into English.

EXAMPLE

هو صديقي وهو يحب _____ كثيراً. <u>هو صديقي وهو يحبني كثيراً.</u>

He is my friend and he likes me very much.

١ هو صديقنا وهو يحب _____ كثيراً.

_____

٢ هو صديقكَ وهو يحب _____ كثيراً.

_____

٣ هو صديقكِ وهو يحب _____ كثيراً.

_____

٤ هو صديقكما وهو يحب _____ كثيراً (d. m.).

_____

٥ هو صديقكما وهو يحب _____ كثيراً (d. f.).

_____

٦ هو صديقكم وهو يحب _____ كثيراً.

_____

٧ هو صديقكن وهو يحب _____ كثيراً.

_____

٨ هو صديقه وهو يحب _____ كثيراً.

_____

٩ هو صديقها وهو يحب _____ كثيراً.

_____

١٠ هو صديقهما وهو يحب _____ كثيراً.

_____

١١ هو صديقهم وهو يحب _____ كثيراً.

_____

١٢ هو صديقهن وهو يحب _____ كثيراً.

_____

The object pronoun "it"

There is no equivalent for the direct object pronoun "it." Thus, nonhuman nouns are referred to by "him" or "her" according to their genders. Both masculine and feminine nonhuman plurals take the direct object pronoun of a third person feminine singular.

EXERCISE

3·2

Rewrite each sentence, replacing the words in boldface with a direct object pronoun. Translate the new sentences into English.

EXAMPLE

قرأنا صحف الصباح معاً. قرأناها معاً.

We read them together.

١ قرأ الكتاب في عطلة عيد الميلاد. _____

_____

٢ اشترت المجلة الأدبية من المكتبة. _____

_____

٣ غسلت الصحون بعد العشاء. _____

_____

٤ شاهدنا فيلماً جميلاً الليلة الماضية. _____

_____

٥ وضعنا الكراسي حول المائدة. _____

_____

٦ تناولنا القهوة بالحليب في الصباح. _____

_____

٧ سأضع الورود في المزهرية. _____

_____

٨ اشترتْ بعض الخضار والفواكه من السوق. _____

_____

٩ طبختْ لهما عشاءً لذيذاً. _____

_____

١٠ تناولا الشاي والكعك في الكافيتريا. _____

_____

Underline the object pronouns and translate the sentences into English.

EXAMPLE   *I gave him the book.* أعطيته الكتاب

١ زملائي يحترمونني كثيراً. _____

٢ يزوروننا كل أحدٍ. _____

٣ أنا أحبكَ كثيراً ياأبي. _____

٤ سنقابلكِ في المقهى يا أمي. _____

٥ نحن لا نعرفكما. _____

٦ رأيتكما في الطريق. _____

٧ سنزوركم غداً. _____

٨ أنتن طالبات ذكيات وأنا أحترمكن. _____

٩ كلمته بالهاتف. _____

١٠ حدثها عن السفر إلى القاهرة. _____

١١ هما جاران لطيفان وأنا أحبهما. _____

١٢ هما صديقتان قديمتان وأنا أعرفهما جيداً. _____

١٣ أنا أحب أصدقائي وأساعدهم. _____

١٤ ١ تصلتُ ببناتها وأخبرتهن عن الحفلة. _____

١٥ نلقاكم قريباً يا سمو الأمير. _____

Rewrite each sentence replacing the word in boldface with a direct object pronoun.

EXAMPLE   تناولنا العشاء تناولناه.

١ أعرف **أسرته** _____

٢ تناولت **القهوة** _____

٣ زاروا **صديقهم** _____

٤ قرأت **المقال** _____

٥ يدرس **العربية** _____

٦ قابلنا **الأستاذة** _____

٧ اشترى **الهدايا** _____

٨ تحترم والديك _____

٩ يساعد الفقراء _____

١٠ كتب رسالتين _____

١١ أحب أخواتي _____

١٢ تشبهين جدتك _____

١٣ يسعدون أولادهم _____

١٤ أغمض عينيه _____

١٥ قابلت صديقاتها _____

١٦ لمحت صديقك _____

١٧ رفعوا العلم _____

١٨ غسلت الصحون _____

١٩ سندعو جيراننا _____

٢٠ ألقت المحاضرة _____

EXERCISE
3·5

Rewrite each sentence, replacing the words in boldface with the appropriate direct object pronoun as in the example. Translate the new sentences into English.

EXAMPLE

كتبت عدة رسائل إلكترونية لأصدقائي في العيد. <u>كتبتها في العيد.</u>

I wrote them on the feast day.

١ سمعنا **الأغنية الجديدة** هذا المساء في النادي. _____

٢ أخبرت **زميلي في الصف** أنني سأذهب إلى المكتبة. _____

٣ سافر إلى بيروت ليقابل **أصدقاء طفولته.** _____

٤ سألَ **الموظفة الجديدة** في قاعة الاستقبال عن موضوع المحاضرة. _____

٥ أنا ذاهبة هذا الصباح لأقابل **مدير الجامعة.** _____

٦ حفظت كل الكلمات الجديدة قبل أن أحضر درس العربية. _____

_____

٧ يا محمد! هل ستذهب يوم الجمعة لتزور جدك وجدتك؟ _____

_____

٨ شاهدنا في السينما يوم السبت الماضي فيلماً أمريكياً طويلاً. _____

_____

٩ اشتريت الأعمال الكاملة لنجيب محفوظ من المكتبة الجديدة. _____

_____

١٠ قرأت السنة الماضية كتاباً عن الحرب العالمية الأولى. _____

_____

١١ أعطيت صديقاتي سلمى وليلى ونجوى كتبي القديمة. _____

_____

١٢ زرعت أشجار ورد جميلة في حديقتي. _____

_____

١٣ ساعد أخته الصغيرة في كتابة الوظيفة. _____

_____

١٤ أخذ عمه وزوجته وأولاده إلى المطعم الصيني. _____

_____

١٥ قرأت المدرسة عدة قصائد للشاعر نزار قباني في الصف. _____

_____

١٦ حدثت جدتي وخالتي وزوج خالتي عن رحلتي إلى المغرب. _____

_____

١٧ وضعت الكتب التي سآخذها إلى الجامعة في الحقيبة. _____

_____

١٨ سيدعو طلابه وطالباته لتناول القهوة معه. _____

_____

١٩ هل رأيتم سيارته وسيارة زوجته الجديدتين واقفتين أمام باب بيتهما؟ _____

_____

First translate each sentence into Arabic and then rewrite the translation, replacing the direct object phrase with a direct object pronoun as in the example.

EXAMPLE   Help your brothers in writing their homework.

ساعد إخوتك في كتابة وظائفهم. ساعدهم في كتابة وظائفهم.

١. I am going to visit my old friend on Friday.

_____

_____

٢. They watched the movie at the university club.

_____

_____

٣. Do you know how to write your name in Arabic?

_____

_____

٤. He bought some red roses for his girlfriend on her birthday.

_____

_____

٥. He likes his colleagues and his students, and they like him very much.

_____

_____

٦. Did you meet the new teacher of Arabic literature?

_____

_____

٧. We asked the (female) employees about the address.

_____

_____

٨. He will invite his new neighbors to the Christmas party.

_____

_____

٩. She made a cake for her fiancé on Valentine's Day.

_____

_____

١٠. Do not wake the children, please!

_____

_____

·4· Prepositional pronouns

Introduction to prepositional pronouns

These are the group of attached pronouns that can be attached like suffixes to most of the Arabic prepositions as a substitute for prepositional nouns. When the preposition is linked to a verb these attached pronouns function like what is called "indirect object pronouns" in English. However, the concept of indirect object does not exist in Arabic and all pronouns that are attached to prepositions are categorized together as a substitute to prepositional nouns.

PLURAL		DUAL		SINGULAR	
us	نا...			me	ي...
you (pl. m.)	كم...	you (d. m. f.)	كما...	you (s. m.)	كَ...
you (pl. f.)	كن...			you (s. f.)	كِ...
them (pl. m.)	هم...	them (d. m.f.)	هما...	him	ه...
them (pl. f.)	هن...			her	ها...

I took the book from the library:	أخذت الكتاب من المكتبة:
I took the book from it.	أخذت الكتاب منها.
I sat in the garden:	جلست في الحديقة:
I sat in it.	جلست فيها.
I called my friends:	اتصلت بأصدقائي:
I called them.	اتصلت بهم.

When the propositions that end with **alif maqsura** ى, which is an inseparable letter, are attached to the prepositional pronouns, the ى turns into a ي.

to you	إلى + ك = إليك

The personal pronoun kum

The pronoun **kum**, which refers to the second person masculine plural, can be used in a very formal situation to address a singular high-profile masculine or feminine personality. This use of the pronoun affects other elements of the sentence—the other elements in the sentence will be put in plural too.

You are welcome, Mr President!	أهلاً بكم يا سيادة الرئيس.

Have/has/own لدى	On على	To إلى
أنا: لديّ	أنا: عليّ	أنا: إليّ
نحن: لدينا	نحن: علينا	نحن: إلينا
أنت: لديك	أنت:عليك	أنت: إليك
أنت: لديك	أنت: عليك	أنت: إليك
أنتما: لديكما	أنتما:عليكما	أنتما: إليكما
أنتما: لديكما	أنتما:عليكما	أنتما: إليكما
أنتم: لديكم	أنتم: عليكم	أنتم: إليكم
أنتن: لديكن	أنتن: عليكن	أنتن: إليكن
هو: لديه	هو: عليه	هو: إليه
هي: لديها	هي: عليها	هي: إليها
هما: لديهما	هما: عليهما	هما: إليهما
هما: لديهما	هما: عليهما	هما: إليهما
هم: لديهم	هم: عليهم	هم: إليهم
هن: لديهن	هن: عليهن	هن: إليهن

Prepositions ending with nun ن

When the propositions that end with a **nūn** ن that has a **sukūn** are attached to the first person plural prepositional pronoun نا, the two letters of ن are joined into one ن with a **shadda**.

$$مِنْ + نا = مِنّا$$

$$عَنْ + نا = عَنّا$$

However, when the propositions that end with a **nūn** ن without a **sukūn** are attached to the first person plural prepositional pronoun نا, the two letters of ن are not joined.

$$بينَ + نا = بيننا$$

$$دونَ + نا = دوننا$$

When the preposition that ends with a ي is attached to the first person singular prepositional pronoun ـي, the two letters of ي are joined in one ي with a **shadda** and a **fatha**.

$$في + ـي = فيَّ$$

Complete these sentences in Arabic by following the English translation.

EXAMPLE   She looked at him and he looked at her. نظرت إليه ونظر _____ •

نظرت إليه ونظر إليها.

١ وضعت ثقتي فيه ووضع ثقته _____ •

I put my trust in him and he put his trust in me.

٢ استعرنا دفاترهم واستعاروا بعض الكتب _____ •

We borrowed their notebooks and they borrowed some books from us.

٣ نسكن بعيداً عن الجامعة والمكتبة أيضاً بعيدة جداً _____ •

We live far from the university and the library is very far from us too.

٤ زرنا أصدقاءهم وسألنا عنهم وزاروا أصدقاءنا وسألوهم _____ •

We visited their friends and asked about them and they visited our friends
and asked them about us.

٥ أخوه يسكن قريباً من أسرتي وهو أيضاً يسكن قريباً _____ •

His brother lives near my family and he also lives near us.

٦ جلست مع صديقي على الأريكة وجلست أخته _____ •

I sat with my friend on the sofa and his sister sat between us.

٧ لا تذهبوا _____ إلى الحفلة. Do not go to the party without us.

٨ _____ موعد مع الطبيب. He has an appointment with the doctor.

Complete each of the following sentences by changing the subject pronoun into
a prepositional pronoun and joining it with the preposition.

EXAMPLE   شعروا بالقلق (على، هو). شعروا بالقلق عليه.

أعدت الكتاب (إلى، أنت). أعدت الكتاب إليك.

١ والدكم يعتمد (على، أنتم) كثيراً. _____

٢ هذان هما الكرسيان اللذان يجلسان (على، هما). _____

٣ فرض (على، أنتن) بعض الواجبات. _____

٤ هطل المطر (على، نحن). _____

٥ يهبط الليل (على، أنت) فجأة. _____

٦ شباكنا يطل (على، هم). _____

٧ شعرنا بالقلق (على، أنتما). _____

٨ طلب منها البقاء ولم يجبرها (على، هو). _____

٩ أغلق (على، أنا) الباب. _____

١٠ حرموا (على، هن) السفر وحيدات. _____

١١ اقترحوا (على، أنت) بعض الحلول. _____

١٢ نثروا الزهور (على، هما). _____

١٣ نظرت (إلى، هو). _____

١٤ جاء (إلى، نحن) أمس. _____

١٥ هو يشير (إلى، أنتِ) يا صديقتي. _____

١٦ سنزور كل الأصدقاء الذين نحلم أن نسافر (إلى، هم). _____

١٧ أرسل (إلى، أنا) وروداً بيضاء. _____

١٨ ذهبوا (إلى، أنتما) بالسيارة. _____

١٩ أهدى (إلى، هما) ألعابا جميلة. _____

٢٠ قدموا (إلى، أنت) بعض الاقتراحات. _____

٢١ سنعود (إلى، أنتن) يا أخواتي. _____

٢٢ اشتاق (إلى، هي). _____

٢٣ استمع (إلى، أنتم) لساعات. _____

٢٤ حملوا (إلى، هن) خبرا ساراً. _____

Combining مع, لـ, and عند with prepositional pronouns

When the prepositions مع, لـ, and عند are combined with prepositional pronouns, they mean "to have," and indicate ownership, possession, and affinities. However, these three combinations have three different functions. Compare these examples:

For both humans and nonhumans:

I have a pen (with me is a pen).	معي قلم.

For nonhuman objects*:

I have a house (I own it).	عندي بيت.

For human relationships:

I have an uncle.	لي عم.

---

*عند is also used for human relations in the Levantine standard Arabic.

When the preposition لـ is combined with prepositional pronouns, it can replace a possessive pronoun and the noun (the possessed object).

This is my book: this is mine.   هذا كتابي: هذا لي.

noun: كتاب

possessive pronoun: ي

replacement of the noun and possessive pronoun: لي

This is your car: this is yours.   هذه سيارتك: هذه لك.

EXERCISE

4·3

Complete the following sentences by changing the subject pronouns into suitable prepositional pronouns, combining the prepositional pronouns with the relevant one of the three prepositions عند, لـ, مع in order to generate the meaning "to have." Translate the new phrases into English.

EXAMPLES

_____ كتاب في الحقيبة. (هو) <u>معه كتاب في الحقيبة.</u>

He has a book in the bag.

_____ بيت كبير. (نحن) <u>عندنا بيت كبير.</u>

We have a big house.

_____ جار طيب. (هما) <u>لهما جار طيب.</u>

They have a good neighbor.

١ _____ كتاب في الحقيبة. (هي)

_____

٢ _____ صديق في طرابلس. (هو)

_____

٣ _____ بيت واسع. (هم)

_____

٤ هل _____ محاضرات هذا المساء؟ (أنتما)

_____

٥ هل _____ كثير من الأصدقاء؟ (أنتم)

_____

٦ _____ شركة تجارية. (هما)

_____

٧ _____ أربعة إخوة. (هي)

_____

٨ ــــــــــــــــــــ دولار في جيبي. (أنا)

_____

٩ ــــــــــــــــــــ خال في أمريكا. (هن)

_____

١٠ ــــــــــــــــــــ قطة وكلب. (هي)

_____

١١ ــــــــــــــــــــ أفكار عظيمة. (أنتن)

_____

١٢ هل ــــــــــــــــــــ أصدقاء في الجامعة؟ (أنت)

_____

١٣ ــــــــــــــــــــ كومبيوتر في السيارة. (هو)

_____

١٤ إنها تمطر، هل ــــــــــــــــــــ مظلة؟ (أنت)

_____

١٥ ليس ــــــــــــــــــــ تلفاز، ولكن عنده راديو؟ (هو)

_____

١٦ أضعت قلمي. هل ــــــــــــــــــــ قلم؟ (أنت)

_____

١٧ كانت ــــــــــــــــــــ حبيبة والآن هو وحيد. (هو)

_____

*Rewrite each sentence, replacing the phrase in boldface with a combination of the
preposition and the prepositional pronoun. Translate the new phrases into English.*

EXAMPLE   سأراك بعد المحاضرة في مطعم الجامعة. سأراك بعد المحاضرة فيه.

I will see you after the lecture there/in it.

١ ذهبت إلى المكتبة لكتابة مقالة عن الشاعر الفلسطيني محمود درويش.

_____

_____

٢ اشتريت كتابي من المكتبة التي كنت قد ذهبت إليها مرة مع أصدقائي.

_____

_____

٣ سأذهب بعد الغداء لأتمشى في حديقة الجامعة.

_____

_____

٤ هل تعرف أن صديقنا سيقضي عيد الميلاد مع والديه؟

_____

_____

٥ لجارتي سبعة أخوة.

_____

_____

٦ عند صديقي بيت كبير وحديقة واسعة.

_____

_____

٧ لدى عائلة صديقي بيت في الريف.

_____

_____

٨ اشتريت صحيفة ومجلة من المحل المجاور لبيتي.

_____

_____

٩ مشينا الأسبوع الماضي إلى الحديقة العامة وجلسنا فيها حتى المساء.

_____

_____

١٠ كتبت وظيفة اللغة العربية بالقلم الجديد الذي اشتريته اليوم.

_____

_____

١١ عندما انتقلنا إلى بيتنا الجديد أقمنا حفلة لنتعرف على جيراننا.

_____

١٢ معظم أصدقائي العرب يجلسون في هذا المقهى.

_____

_____

The preposition على

When the preposition على is attached to the prepositional pronouns, and followed by a noun or a verbal phrase, it means "must," "should," or "have to."

على + ي: عليَّ الذهاب إلى المكتبة.

عليَّ أن أذهب إلى المكتبة.

I have to go to the library.

EXERCISE
4·5

Rewrite each sentence, replacing the preposition and the subject pronoun in parentheses with a combination of the preposition and the prepositional pronoun. Translate your sentences into English.

EXAMPLE

(على، أنا) أن أطبخ الغداء، وعليكم إعداد المائدة. <u>عليَّ أن أطبخ الغداء وعليكم إعداد المائدة.</u>

I have to cook dinner and you have to set the table.

١ (على، أنا) الدراسة قبل الامتحان. _____

_____

٢ (على، نحن) الذهاب إلى السوق لشراء الطعام. _____

_____

٣ (على، أنتم) احترام والديكم. _____

_____

٤ (على، هما) قراءة صحف اليوم. _____

_____

٥ (على، أنت) تنظيف البيت. _____

_____

٦ (على، أنت) غسل الصحون. _____

_____

٧ (على أنتما) التفكير في المستقبل. _____

_____

٨ (على أنتم) حفظ الكلمات الجديدة. _____

_____

٩ (على، هو) كتابة الوظيفة. _____

_____

١٠ (على، هي) كتابة التمارين. _____

_____

Prepositional pronouns **39**

١١ (على، أنتن) زيارة جدتكن.

_____

_____

١٢ (على، هم) أخذ خالتهم إلى الطبيب.

_____

_____

١٣ (على، أنا) شراء هدية لصديقي.

_____

_____

١٤ (على، هن) مساعدة أسرتهن في الإعداد للحفلة.

_____

_____

EXERCISE
4·6

First translate each sentence into Arabic and then rewrite the Arabic translation, replacing the indirect object phrase with a prepositional pronoun.

EXAMPLE   الأستاذ ينتظر في مكتبه. The teacher is waiting in his office.

الأستاذ ينتظر فيه.

١ Today is the exam of Arabic language at the university.

_____

_____

٢ The students go to the university library at nine o'clock in the morning.

_____

_____

٣ The students enter the exam hall at ten o'clock.

_____

_____

٤ The students sit on the wooden seats.

_____

_____

٥ They put their books in their bags.

_____

_____

They write their names with their pens. ٦

_____

_____

The teacher takes out the names notebook from his bag. ٧

_____

_____

The teacher reads the students' names in his notebook. ٨

_____

_____

The teacher gives the exam papers to the students. ٩

_____

_____

The students write answers to the questions. ١٠

_____

_____

When they finish they put all the papers in front of the teacher. ١١

_____

_____

The students exit the exam hall at one o'clock. ١٢

_____

_____

They walk and then they enter the Arabic café with their friends. ١٣

_____

_____

They drink Arabian coffee and speak about the exam. ١٤

_____

_____

·5· Pronouns and other particles

Particles

In Chapter 4 we reviewed the combinations of prepositions and attached pronouns. There are other particles that can similarly be followed by a noun or a pronoun. These particles take the same attached pronouns as the prepositions. These include إنَّ, and أنَّ, كأنَّ, ليت, لعل, لكنَّ.

This group is called "أنَّ and its sisters." They are also called "verb-like letters" and they precede nominal sentences.

إنَّ: An emphatic article that introduces a sentence. It has no equivalent in English when it comes at the beginning of a sentence.

The weather is cold . . . It is cold.	إنَّ الطقس بارد ... إنَّه بارد.

إنَّ also follows the verb قال "to say."

He said that the students were hardworking . . . He said that they were hardworking.	قال إنَّ الطلاب مجتهدون ... قال إنَّهم مجتهدون.

أنَّ: This is a conjunction that is equivalent to "that." It follows certain verbs.

I know that the study is difficult . . . I know it is difficult.	أعرف أنَّ الدراسة صعبة ... أعرف أنَّها صعبة.

لكنَّ: It means "however," "but," or "yet."

She agreed but her friend refused . . . She agreed but he refused.	وافقت لكنَّ صديقها رفض ... وافقت لكنَّه رفض.

كأنَّ: It means "as if," "like," or "as though."

The day passed slowly as if the day were a year . . . The day passed slowly as if it were a year.	مر اليوم ببطء وكأنَّ اليوم سنة ... مر اليوم ببطء وكأنَّه سنة.

لعل: It means "maybe" or "perhaps."

Let's go! Maybe the café is open . . . Let's go! Maybe it is open.	فلنذهب! لعل المقهى مفتوح ... فلنذهب! لعله مفتوح.

ليت: It means "if only."

I wish my friend were with me . . .	ليت صديقي معي ...
I wish he were with me.	ليته معي.

Another group of particles is the "the particles of exception" such as سوى, إلا.

Nobody called except Khalid . . .	لم يتصل أحد إلا خالد ...
Nobody called except him.	لم يتصل إلاه.
Nobody attended except Walid . . .	لم يحضر أحد سوى وليد ...
Nobody attended except him.	لم يحضر سواه.

These particles can be followed by the following attached pronouns:

PLURAL		DUAL		SINGULAR	
we	...نا			I	ي...
you (pl. m.)	...كم	you (d. m. f.)	...كما	you (s. m.)	ك...
you (pl. f.)	...كن			you (s. f.)	ك...
they (pl. m.)	...هم	they (d. m. f.)	...هما	he	ه...
they (pl. f.)	...هن			she	ها...

And they will then produce the combinations with the subject pronouns.

أنا: إنّي (إنّني)، أنّي (أنّني)، لكنّي (لكنّني)، كأنّي (كأنّني)، لعلي (لعلني)، ليتني، إلاي، سواي

نحن: إنّنا، أنّنا، لكنّنا، كأنّنا، لعلنا، ليتنا، إلانا، سوانا

أنتَ: إنّكَ، أنّكَ، لكنّكَ، كأنّكَ، لعلكِ، ليتكِ، إلاكَ، سواك

أنتِ: إنّكِ، أنّكِ، لكنّكِ، كأنّكِ، لعلكِ، ليتكِ، إلاكِ، سواك

أنتما: إنّكما، أنّكما، لكنّكما، كأنّكما، لعلكما، ليتكما، إلاكما، سواكما

أنتما: إنّكما، أنّكما، لكنّكما، كأنّكما، لعلكما، ليتكما، إلاكما، سواكما

أنتم: إنّكم، أنّكم، لكنّكم، كأنّكم، لعلكم، ليتكم، إلاكم، سواكم

أنتن: إنّكن، أنّكن، لكنّكن، كأنّكن، لعلكن، ليتكن، إلاكن، سواكن

هو: إنّه، أنّه، لكنّه، كأنّه، لعله، ليته، إلاه، سواه

هي: إنّها، أنّها، لكنّها، كأنّها، لعلها، ليتها، إلاها، سواها

هما: إنّهما، أنّهما، لكنّهما، كأنّهما، لعلهما، ليتهما، إلاهما، سواهما

هما: إنّهما، أنّهما، لكنّهما، كأنّهما، لعلهما، ليتهما، إلاهما، سواهما

هم: إنّهم، أنّهم، لكنّهم، كأنّهم، لعلهم، ليتهم، إلاهم، سواهم

هن: إنّهن، أنّهن، لكنّهن، كأنّهن، لعلهن، ليتهن، إلاهن، سواهن

Translate the following sentences into English.

EXAMPLES
كتب لها ولكنها لم تجب. *He wrote to her but she did not reply.*

أظن أن دراسة اللغات ممتعة جداً. *I think that studying languages is very interesting.*

١ إنّ الطالبات في مكتبة الجامعة. _____

٢ يتصرفون وكأنّهم في بيتهم. _____

٣ فتح الرسالة وقرأها، ولكنّه لم يفهمها. _____

٤ إنّ الطالبين مصريان من مدينة الإسكندرية. _____

٥ لعلهم يخبرونها. _____

٦ إنّ الطالبتين سوريتان من مدينة طرطوس. _____

٧ أشعر أنّك صديق حقيقي. _____

٨ ليتهم يفهمون. _____

٩ إنّ الطلاب في الصف. _____

١٠ أعرف أنّك ستسافر غداً. _____

١١ إنّ الشارع واسع. _____

١٢ انتظرنا لكنّهم لم يأتوا. _____

١٣ لا أحد يمكنه القيام بالمهمة إلاك. _____

١٤ مر اليوم بسرعة وكأنّه ساعة. _____

١٥ انتظر لعلهم قادمون. _____

١٦ إنّ المكتبة مفتوحة حتى الساعة السابعة مساء. _____

١٧ حضر الجميع إلاكما. _____

١٨ دعونا الأهل والأصدقاء ولم يحضر سواهم. _____

١٩ ليتك كنت هنا. _____

٢٠ الطفل جميل كأنّه ملاك حين يبتسم. _____

Each of the following sentences includes one of the following particles:

لعل	كأنّ	لكنّ (ولكنّ)	أنّ	إنّ
سوى	إلا	يا ليت	ليت	

and is followed by a noun. Change the noun after each of these particles into an attached pronoun and translate your new phrases into English.

إن مكتبة الجامعة بعيدة عن بيتي. <u>إنها بعيدة عن بيتي.</u>

It is far from my home.

١ سأذهب إلى الكافيتيريا لعل أصدقائي يجلسون هناك.

_____

_____

٢ قالت لنا إنّ المدير سيؤجل اجتماع اليوم إلى الأسبوع القادم.

_____

_____

٣ قرعنا على بابكم هذا الصباح، ولكنّ أمكم لم تكن في البيت.

_____

_____

٤ الغرفة باردة ... كأنّ درجة الحرارة صفر هنا.

_____

_____

٥ أعرف أنّك تحبني وأنّ أهلك مثل أهلي.

_____

_____

٦ لم أتعرف على أي طالب إلّا الطالبين اللذين جلسا بجانبي.

_____

_____

٧ أحتاج لبعض المساعدة في نقل كتبي إلى غرفتي الجديدة، ولكنّ كل صديقاتي مشغولات.

_____

_____

٨ إنّ الموظفين سيأخذون إجازات أطول هذه السنة.

_____

_____

٩ ليت الأستاذ يعطينا وظائف أسهل.

_____

_____

١٠ لم يحضر الفيلم في النادي إلّا عشرة طلاب.

_____

_____

The particle أنّ

أنّ is a conjunction that introduces a sentence complement. It is the Arabic equivalent of "that," which follows some verbs that are used to report information. The most commonly used verbs that are followed by أنّ are:

knew that	عرف أنّ
read that	قرأ أنّ
heard that	سمع أنّ
felt that	شعر أنّ
sensed that, felt that	أحس أنّ
had knowledge (was informed) that	علم أنّ
understood that	فهم أنّ
means that	يعني أنّ
remembered that	تذكر أنّ
imagined that	تصور أنّ
thought, reckoned that	ظن أنّ
believed, thought that	اعتقد أنّ

However, there is one verb that takes إنّ:

said that	قال إنّ

أنّ turns into إنّ when it follows the verb "to say" to indicate a quotable saying.

قال إنّ اللغة العربية الكلاسيكية صعبة ... أعرف أنّها صعبة.

Translate the following sentences into Arabic.

EXAMPLES   لم يعرف أنها قرأت كتابه الأخير. He did not know that she has read his last book.

عرفت أنه قرأ كتابي. I knew that he has read my book.

They understood that he was happy with the meeting. ١

_____

We read in the newspapers that they are facing difficulties in reaching an agreement. ٢

_____

She read the letter but this does not mean that she will send a reply. ٣

_____

They did not imagine that you would accept. ٤

_____

Do you believe that the situation will change? ٥

_____

She feels that he is trying to get closer to her. ٦

_____

They assumed that she would return. ٧

_____

I knew that he wanted to change his job. ٨

_____

She remembered that he had promised to do that. ٩

_____

They said that you would finally solve the problem. ١٠

_____

He did not know that the exams were delayed because of the snow. ١١

_____

She sensed that he wanted to get to know her. ١٢

_____

The structure of the last sentence in Exercise 5.2 is called "reported speech." Change the following statements into reported speech as in the example.

EXAMPLE سأتصل بك كل مساء. قال لها إنّه سيتصل بها كل مساء.

١ نحن سعيدان.

قال لهم _____

٢ سأسافر لزيارة أقاربي.

قالت لك _____

٣ أنا أحب أن أساعد زملائي في واجباتهم.

قال لي _____

٤ سأزور جدتي يوم الأحد.

سيقولان له _____

٥ كنا ندرس في المكتبة القريبة من جامعتنا.

قالوا لنا _____

٦ نحن صديقتان منذ الطفولة ونسكن في نفس الحي.

قالتا لها _____

٧ نرغب في زيارة كل الأماكن التي قرأنا عنها في الكتب.

سنقول لهم _____

٨ أنا البنت الوحيدة في الصف ومعي خمسة طلاب.

قالت لهما _____

٩ نحن طالبات اللغة العربية ولكننا ندرس التاريخ ولغات أخرى.

قلن لي _____

١٠ سأتصل بخطيبتي مها لأننا سنسافر معاً إلى دمشق والقاهرة وسنأخذ معنا بعض الهدايا لأصدقائنا.

سيقول لهم _____

Demonstrative pronouns ·6·

Demonstrative pronouns in Arabic are divided into two major categories: demonstratives of proximity and demonstratives of distance. These are used for close nouns and for far nouns, respectively.

Demonstrative pronouns of proximity

The demonstratives for close nouns are:

this (s. m.) هذا	
this ([s. f.] and for nonhuman plural) هذه	
these ([d. m.] nominative) هذان	
these ([d. m.] accusative and genitive) هذين	
these ([d. f.] nominative) هاتان	
these ([d. f.] accusative and genitive and for nonhumans) هاتين	
these ([pl. m. f.] for humans only) هؤلاء	

This house is big.	هذا البيت كبير.
This room is small.	هذه الغرفة صغيرة.
These two men are Egyptians.	هذان الرجلان مصريان.
I met these two (male) teachers.	قابلت هذين الأستاذين.
These two girls are Algerians.	هاتان البنتان جزائريتان.
I met these two female students.	قابلت هاتين الطالبتين.
These boys are playing football.	هؤلاء الأولاد يلعبون كرة القدم.
These girls speak Arabic.	هؤلاء الفتيات يتكلمن العربية.

Note that whereas there is a demonstrative article for human plural, nonhuman plural takes the singular feminine demonstrative article. Compare the following with the previous examples:

These books are new.	هذه الكتب جديدة.
These newspapers are old.	هذه الجرائد قديمة

Complete these sentences by writing the appropriate proximity demonstrative pronouns for the nouns in boldface. Translate the sentences into English.

EXAMPLE   ــــــــــــــــــــــــــــــ **طالب جديد.** هذا طالب جديد.

This is a new student.

١ ــــــــــــــــــــــــ **الأستاذ يدرس اللغة العربية.**

ـــ

٢ ــــــــــــــــــــــــ **الأستاذة تسكن في لندن.**

ـــ

٣ ــــــــــــــــــــــــ **الأطباء يعملون في المشفى.**

ـــ

٤ ــــــــــــــــــــــــ **الكتابان على الطاولة.**

ـــ

٥ وضعت ــــــــــــــــــــــــ **الكتابين في الحقيبة.**

ـــ

٦ ــــــــــــــــــــــــ **المجلتان على الرف.**

ـــ

٧ قرأت ــــــــــــــــــــــــ **المجلتين.**

ـــ

٨ ــــــــــــــــــــــــ **الكتب من المكتبة.**

ـــ

٩ اشتريت ــــــــــــــــــــــــ **المجلات أمس.**

ـــ

Demonstrative pronouns of distance

The demonstrative pronouns that show distance are:

ذلك that ([s. m.])

تلك that ([s. f.] and for nonhuman plural)

ذانك those ([d. m.] nominative)

ذينك those ([d. m.] accusative and genitive)

those ([d. f.] nominative) تانك

those ([d. f.] accusative and genitive) تينك

those ([pl. f. m.] for human only) أولئك

Note that ذاك is a demonstrative for distance and it is a variation of ذلك. It is more classical and is used in modern standard Arabic, especially for contrast with هذا.

There is a big difference between this and that.	هناك فرق كبير بين هذا وذاك.
Compare this to that.	قارن هذا بذاك.
That street is long.	ذلك الشارع طويل.
That city is far.	تلك المدينة بعيدة.
Those two boys are clever.	ذانك الولدان ذكيان.
I read those two books.	قرأت ذينك الكتابين.
Those two journals are famous.	تانك المجلتان شهيرتان.
I know those two girls.	أعرف تينك البنتين.
Those boys work in the field.	أولئك الأولاد يعملون في الحقل.
Those women work in the factory.	أولئك النساء يعملن في المعمل.

The same rule, as for nonhuman plural, applies for demonstratives for distant nouns. Nonhuman plurals are treated like singular feminine. Compare the following sentences:

That girl is smart.	تلك البنت ذكية.
Those streets are long.	تلك الشوارع طويلة.

EXERCISE

6·2

Fill in the blanks with the appropriate distance demonstrative pronouns. Translate the completed sentences into English.

EXAMPLE   كتبت بـ ــــــــــــــــــ القلم. كتبت بذاك القلم.

I wrote with that pen.

١ استمتعت بـ ــــــــــــــــــ القصة.

_____

٢ نحب ــــــــــــــــــ الجيران.

_____

٣ جلسنا في ــــــــــــــــــ المقهى.

_____

٤ ـــــــــــــــــــــــ الأستاذتان تدرسان العربية.

_____

٥ تعرفنا على ـــــــــــــــــــــــ الزميلين الجديدين.

_____

٦ حدثها عن ـــــــــــــــــــــــ الخطة وعن ـــــــــــــــــــــــ القرار.

_____

٧ ذهبوا إلى ـــــــــــــــــــــــ الحديقة العامة.

_____

٨ ـــــــــــــــــــــــ السيارات غالية.

_____

٩ خرج من ـــــــــــــــــــــــ الباب.

_____

١٠ قرأت ـــــــــــــــــــــــ المجلتين.

_____

١١ ـــــــــــــــــــــــ الكتابان ممتعان.

_____

١٢ ـــــــــــــــــــــــ الأفلام قديمة.

_____

١٣ ـــــــــــــــــــــــ المدن بعيدة.

_____

Demonstratives can be followed by both indefinite and definite nouns. Compare the following sentences:

This is a book.	هذا كتاب.
That is a magazine.	تلك مجلة.
This is an Arabic newspaper.	هذه جريدة عربية.
This book is new.	هذا الكتاب جديد.
That Arabic newspaper is old.	تلك الجريدة العربية قديمة.
These are new students.	هؤلاء طلاب جدد.
Those students are new.	أولئك الطلاب جدد. الطلاب جدد.
These new students are smart.	هؤلاء الطلاب الجدد أذكياء.

Translate the following sentences into Arabic.

EXAMPLE   هذا الكتاب جديد. This book is new.

This is a bus. ١

_____

This is a small car. ٢

_____

This bus is big. ٣

_____

This small car is new. ٤

_____

This is a boy. ٥

_____

This is a girl. ٦

_____

This boy is happy. ٧

_____

This girl is beautiful. ٨

_____

This little boy is happy. ٩

_____

This little girl is beautiful. ١٠

_____

These are happy boys. ١١

_____

These are very beautiful girls. ١٢

_____

These boys are very happy. ١٣

_____

These girls are very beautiful. ١٤

_____

These little boys are very happy. ١٥

_____

These little girls are very beautiful. ١٦

_____

Definite predicates

The predicates in the previous examples of Arabic sentences are indefinite. If the predicate is definite, the demonstrative should be followed by a subject pronoun that agrees with it in gender and number. This applies to both demonstratives—proximity and distance.

This is the river.	هذا هو النهر.
That is the city.	تلك هي المدينة.
These are the successful students.	هؤلاء هم الطلاب الناجحون.

EXERCISE
6·4

Complete the following sentences by deriving the appropriate demonstrative pronoun—distance or proximity—and the subject pronouns. Translate the new sentences into English.

EXAMPLES
صديقي المفضل. <u>هذا هو صديقي المفضل.</u> _____

This is my best friend.

المقالة الطويلة. <u>هذه هي المقالة الطويلة.</u> _____

This is the long article.

١ _____ المدينة القديمة.

_____

٢ _____ الأطفال السعداء.

_____

٣ _____ دفاتر الولد وأقلامه.

_____

٤ _____ ثياب البنت وألعابها.

_____

٥ _____ النادي الجامعي.

_____

٦ _____ حديقة الجامعة.

_____

٧ _____ أشجار الياسمين.

_____

٨ _____ الكتاب الجديد.

_____

٩ _____ وزير التعليم.

_____

١٠ _____ طلاب السنة الثالثة.

_____

١١ _____ طالبات السنة الأولى.

_____

١٢ _____ مدراء الجامعات الخاصة.

_____

١٣ _____ الأستاذان الجديدان.

_____

١٤ _____ السكرتيرتان اللطيفتان.

_____

١٥ _____ المطعم الشامي.

_____

١٦ _____ الأطباق اللذيذة.

_____

١٧ _____ المشروبات الباردة.

_____

١٨ _____ طاولتنا المفضلة.

_____

Demonstrative pronouns that change meaning

When some demonstrative pronouns are combined with certain prepositions or articles they acquire new meanings. This applies to both demonstratives of proximity and demonstratives of distance. The most commonly used ones include:

in spite of that, nevertheless	مع هذا، مع ذلك
thereafter, after that	بعد هذا، بعد ذلك
so, thus, for this reason, therefore	لهذا، لذلك
equally, likewise, in that manner	كذلك

Complete each phrase in list A with the appropriate complement from list B. Translate your answers into English.

B	A
ولهذا لن أذهب إلى الحديقة.	هذا فيلم جميل
وأنتِ كذلك صديقتي.	الطقس بارد
مع هذا لن أشاهده لأن عندي وظيفة.	كان متعباً
وبعد هذا سنتناول القهوة.	هو صديقي
وبعد ذلك سيذهبون إلى المقهى.	عندي امتحان غداً
ومع ذلك لعب كرة القدم مع أصدقائه.	سنتناول الغداء
ولذلك سأدرس طوال الليل.	سيذهبون إلى المكتبة

١ _____

٢ _____

٣ _____

٤ _____

٥ _____

٦ _____

٧ _____

Relative pronouns

Introduction to relative pronouns

These are a group of pronouns that are used to link phrases, clauses, and sentences. A relative clause refers to a noun that is called the antecedent or the topical noun, and the noun must be a definite noun.

The relative pronouns agree with the antecedent in gender and number.

The student who studies Arabic is my friend (s. m.).	الطالب الذي يدرس العربية صديقي.
The (female) student who studies Arabic is my friend (s. f.).	الطالبة التي تدرس العربية صديقتي.
The two students who study Arabic are my friends (d. m.).	الطالبان اللذان يدرسان العربية صديقاي.
The two (female) students who study Arabic are my friends (d. f.).	الطالبتان اللتان تدرسان العربية صديقتاي.
The students who study Arabic are my friends (pl. m.).	الطلاب الذين يدرسون العربية أصدقائي.
The (female) students who study Arabic are my friends (pl. f.).	الطالبات اللواتي يدرسن العربية صديقاتي.

The relative pronoun for the dual form agrees with the antecedent in gender, number, and status of duality. In the accusative and genitive cases, the relative pronouns for the dual take the following forms:

who, which, whom, that, what, whose (d. m.) اللذين

Note that if the dual being described consists of a female and a male, then this relative pronoun اللذين is used.

who, which, whom, that, what, whose (d. f.) اللتين

I know the two students who study Arabic.	أعرف الطالبين اللذين يدرسان العربية.
I know the two (female) students who study Arabic.	أعرف الطالبتين اللتين تدرسان العربية.

Nonhuman plurals take the relative pronoun of the singular feminine.

<table>
<tr><td>I bought some books that are issued
by Oxford University Press.</td><td dir="rtl">اشتريت بعض الكتب التي صدرت عن
مطبعة جامعة أكسفورد.</td></tr>
</table>

EXERCISE
7·1

Complete these sentences by writing the appropriate relative pronouns for the nouns in boldface. Translate the new sentences into English.

EXAMPLE القصة ـــــــــــــــــــــ قرأتها جميلة جداً. القصة التي قرأتها جميلة جداً.

The story that I have read is very beautiful.

١ البيت ـــــــــــــــــــــ يقع قرب النهر جميل جداً.

_____

٢ الحديقة ـــــــــــــــــــــ تحيط بالبيت جميلة جداً.

_____

٣ الرجل ـــــــــــــــــــــ يسكن في هذا البيت صديقي.

_____

٤ العجوزان ـــــــــــــــــــــ يسكنان معه هما والداه.

_____

٥ السيدتان ـــــــــــــــــــــ تزورانهم أحيانا هما خالتاه.

_____

٦ المرأة ـــــــــــــــــــــ تزورهم كل يوم هي أخته.

_____

٧ والأطفال ـــــــــــــــــــــ يقضون معهم يوم الأحد هم أولاد أخته.

_____

٨ زرت صديقي ووالديه ـــــــــــــــــــــ يسكنان معه.

_____

٩ وتعرفت على خالتيه ـــــــــــــــــــــ تزورانه أحياناً.

_____

Referent pronouns

When the topical noun is not the subject of the verb that follows the relative pronoun, the antecedent will be the object of this verb. Accordingly, the verb refers to a different subject. In the standard mainstream Arabic grammar, this verb takes a pronoun in the relative clause referring to the antecedent. This pronoun is called the referent pronoun or the presumptive pronoun. Look at the following example where the antecedent is in boldface and the relative clause is underlined.

The student whom I visited is my friend.

الطالب الذي زرته صديقي.

the antecedent: الطالب

the relative clause: الذي زرته

referent pronoun: ه

When the verb takes a preposition, the presumptive (referent) pronoun should be attached to the preposition.

The student whom I live with is my friend.

الطالب الذي أسكن معه صديقي.

the antecedent: الطالب

the relative clause: الذي أسكن معه

referent pronoun: ه

EXERCISE
7·2

Write the appropriate referent pronouns for the following verbs in boldface. Translate the new sentences into English.

EXAMPLE

هذا هو صديقي الذي أحب. هذا هو صديقي الذي أحبه.

This is my friend, whom I love.

١ هذه هي المقالة التي قرأت. _____

_____

٢ هذه هي القصة التي استمتعت بـ. _____

_____

٣ هؤلاء هم الأصدقاء الذين سافرنا مع. _____

_____

٤ هذه هي الموظفة التي اتصلنا بـ. _____

_____

٥ هذا هو المطعم الذي تغدينا في. _____

_____

٦ هذا هو الثوب الذي اشترت. ــــــــــــــــــــ
ـــ

٧ هذا هو الأستاذ الذي أعجبت بـ. ـــــــــــــــ
ـــ

٨ هذه هي الأشجار التي مشينا بين. ـــــــــــــ
ـــ

٩ هذه هي المظلة التي جلسنا تحت. ـــــــــــــ
ـــ

١٠ هذا هو النهر الذي سبحتم فيـ. ـــــــــــــــ
ـــ

١١ هذه هي البحيرة التي لعبوا حولـ. ـــــــــــ
ـــ

١٢ هذا هو الجسر الذي عبرو. ـــــــــــــــــــ
ـــ

١٣ هذه هي الموسيقى التي استمعنا إلى. ـــــــــ
ـــ

١٤ هذا هو القلم الذي كتبنا بـ. ــــــــــــــــــ
ـــ

Adjectival sentences

When the topical noun of the relative clause is an indefinite noun, a relative pronoun is not used. The relative clause will follow the topical noun directly like adjectives follow nouns in Arabic. Therefore, this type of descriptive sentence is called **jumlat al-sifa** in Arabic or "the adjectival sentence." Compare the following sentences:

I met the guy who studies Arabic.	قابلت الشاب الذي يدرس العربية.
I met a guy who studies Arabic.	قابلت شاباً يدرس العربية.

If the topical noun is followed by another noun, the second noun will have an attached referent pronoun that points to the topical noun.

I met a girl whose name is Amira.	قابلت فتاةً اسمها أميرة.

topical noun: فتاة

the adjectival sentence: اسمها أميرة

the referent pronoun: ـها

We know a teacher whose name is Walid.   نعرف أستاذاً اسمه وليد.

topical noun: أستاذاً

the adjectival sentence: اسمه وليد

the referent pronoun: ـه

If the topical noun is the direct object or the indirect object of the verb, i.e., it is not the subject of the verb, and the verb has a different subject, then the verb will also take a referent attached pronoun, which points to the topical noun.

She heard news that made her happy.   سمعت خبراً أسعدها.

topical noun: خبراً

the adjectival sentence: أسعدها

the referent pronoun: ـها

Today we met a friend whom we got   قابلنا اليوم صديقاً تعرفنا عليه في دمشق.
      to know in Damascus.

topical noun: صديقاً

the adjectival sentence: تعرفنا عليه في دمشق

the referent pronoun: ـه

The following list includes sentences with relative clauses and those that include adjectival sentences. Identify the relative-clause sentences by filling in the blanks with the appropriate pronouns and identify adjectival sentences by marking the blanks with a ✓.

EXAMPLES   قرأت المقالة التي تحدث عبم حقوق النساء.

قرأت مقالة ✓ تتحدث عن حقوق النساء.

١ سمير هو الزميل _____ أعمل معه.

٢ زرنا عائلة _____ تسكن في قريتنا.

٣ السيارة _____ تقف أمام باب بيته هي سيارة والده.

٤ هذه هي الشركة _____ يعمل بها.

٥ هذا هو الكتاب _____ يتكون من ١٤ فصلاً.

٦ هذا أذكى شاب _____ قابلته في حياتي.

٧ تلقيت هدية _____ فرحت بها كثيراً.

٨ هذه هي الجامعة _____ ندرس بها.

٩ هذا أسعد يوم _____ عشته في حياتي.

١٠ سأزور هذا الصيف أصدقائي _____ يدرسون في جامعة حلب.

١١ قابلت البنت _____ تدعى سلمى.

١٢ سقى وروداً _____ زرعها في الحديقة.

١٣ سمعت كلاماً _____ أسعدني.

١٤ قابل في الحفلة _____ امرأة أعجب بها.

١٥ سأزور مدينة تدمر لأرى معبد بعل _____ رأينا صوره في كتاب التاريخ.

١٦ "علاء الدين" فيلم مشهور _____ أنتجته شركة ديزني.

EXERCISE
7·4

Rewrite these sentences and use the relevant relative pronouns to turn their adjectival clauses into relative clauses.

EXAMPLE

هذا كتاب قرأته في العطلة. (This is a book I read on vacation.)

<u>هذا هو الكتاب الذي قرأته في العطلة.</u> (This is the book that I read on vacation.)

١ هذه مقالة مهمة حدثتك عنها أمس.

_____

٢ تعرفنا في مدينة تدمر على سياح جاؤوا لزيارة معبد بعل.

_____

٣ هو صديق أتكلم معه عن مشاكلي وأحلامي.

_____

٤ حدثنا عن فيلم شاهده في نادي الجامعة.

_____

٥ دعت موظفتين تعملان معها في نفس المكتب إلى الحفلة.

_____

٦ أرسلت بطاقات إلكترونية في رأس السنة لطالبات درسن معي في الجامعة.

_____

٧ أهداني صديقي كتاباً كنت أتمنى دوماً الحصول عليه.

_____

٨ هذه رواية ممتعة يمكن أن تعجب كل من يقرأها.

_____

٩ اشترينا بيتا كنا نحلم به دوما ونتمنى أن نسكنه.

_____

١٠ زرنا مطعماً قدم لنا أطباقاً عربية لذيذة.

_____

١١ هؤلاء أصدقاء سافرنا معهم إلى سوريا الشهر الماضي.

_____

١٢ التقيت في الشارع بنتا تسكن عائلتها البيت المقابل لبيت أهلي وسلمت عليها.

_____

Relative pronouns of nonspecific statements

"What/whatever" and "who/whoever" (ما and من, respectively) are separate categories of relative pronouns that imply their antecedents. Thus, they cannot be preceded by antecedents. In contrast to the pronouns of the first category of الذي and its group, which are used in specific statements, these two pronouns are used in general, nonspecific statements and function like "the person that" and "the thing that," respectively.

I did not understand what he said.   لم أفهم ما قال.

We do not know who is going to   لا نعرف من سيزورنا هذه الجمعة.
visit us this Friday.

EXERCISE
7·5

Complete the following sentences by adding one of the relative pronouns of nonspecific statements.

EXAMPLES   أحب _____ يحبني. أحب من يحبني

سآكل _____ أريد. سآكل ما أريد.

١ كل _____ يعرفها يحبها.

٢ هي تعرف كل _____ يفكر به.

٣ لا أعرف _____ تعنيه هذه الكلمة بالعربية.

٤ يريد أن يحدثها عن كل _____ يشعر به.

٥ سنقول له _____ يرغب بسماعه.

٦ على _____ يريد أن يتعلم عن الثقافة العربية أن يعيش في بلد عربي.

٧ لا أعرف من تابع دراسته _____ زملائي، أو _____ وجد وظيفة.

First translate each sentence into Arabic and then rewrite the translation, replacing the relative pronouns that are used in specific statements (along with their antecedents) with one of the two pronouns that are used in general, nonspecific statements.

EXAMPLE I love the person who loves me. أحب الشخص الذي يحبني.

أحب من يحبني.

1. I told him about all the paintings that I have seen in the exhibition.

_____

_____

2. They told us about all the students whom they met at the party.

_____

_____

3. He told his mother about all the stories that he read in Arabic literature class.

_____

_____

4. She told her (female) friends about all the news that she has heard in the market.

_____

_____

5. They respect all the people who respect them.

_____

_____

6. He told his friends about all the countries that he decided to visit in the future.

_____

_____

7. The university announced that it will give scholarships to all the poor students who need them.

_____

_____

8. Are you going to send Christmas cards to all the colleagues who work with you at the company?

_____

_____

She very well remembers all the novels that she read in her childhood. ٩

_____

_____

If you stop studying the Arabic language now, you will forget most of the words ١٠

that you have learned.

_____

_____

I put all the clothes that I will take along on my trip in my suitcase. ١١

_____

_____

I visited all my friends with whom I studied in the secondary school. ١٢

_____

_____

·8· Interrogative pronouns

This group of particles can be divided into two major categories according to their functions: information question particles and yes-no question particles.

Information question particles

Information question particles are particles that seek specific information. Unlike the structure of English questions, the structure of the Arabic question has the same word order of the statement and there is no inversion in any part of the sentence.

Information question particles are further divided into single particles and compound particles.

Single particles

This group includes the following question particles:

what? (in questions without verbs) ما؟

What is this?	ما هذا؟
What is your name?	ما اسمك؟

what? (in questions with verbs) ماذا؟

What is he doing?	ماذا يفعل؟
What are you reading?	ماذا تقرأ؟

who? whom? من؟

Who are his friends?	من أصدقاؤه؟
Whom are you going to invite to the party?	من ستدعو للحفلة؟

where? أين؟

Where do you live?	أين تسكنون؟
Where is your car?	أين سيارتك؟

when? متى؟

When is the party?	متى الحفلة؟
When will the class start?	متى سيبدأ الدرس؟

how? كيف؟

How is the family?

كيف العائلة؟

How was your holiday?

كيف كانت عطلتك؟

which? أيّ؟

Which book is your book?

أي كتاب كتابك؟

how much? how many? كم؟

How many books do you have?

كم كتاباً عندك؟

How much do you love your country?

كم تحب بلدك؟

Compound particles

These particles combine a question particle with a preposition. This group includes, but is not limited to, the following particles:

why? (literally: for what reason?) لماذا؟

Why are you laughing?

لماذا تضحكون؟

how much? (literally: with how much? for questions about price and value) بكم؟

How much is a kilo of oranges?

بكم كيلو البرتقال؟

How much did you buy your ring for?

بكم اشتريت خاتمك؟

where from? من أين؟

Where are you from?

من أين أنت؟

Where did you buy the book from?

من أين اشتريت الكتاب؟

in which? at which? في أيّ؟

At which university do you study?

في أي جامعة تدرس؟

who with? مع من؟

Who do you play football with on Friday?

مع من تلعب كرة القدم يوم الجمعة؟

where to? where? إلى أين؟

Where are you going (going to) after class?

إلى أين ستذهب بعد الدرس؟

until when? how long? إلى متى؟

Until when are we going to wait for them at the station?

إلى متى سننتظرهم في المحطة؟

how much? how much of? كم من؟

How much money do you need?

كم من النقود تحتاج؟

The English question word what is used for both verbal and nominal questions. In Arabic, there are two different question articles for verbal and nominal questions. Use the appropriate particle to complete the questions of the following answers. Translate the questions into English.

EXAMPLE

اسمه "الفردوس" وشربت فيه قهوة. ــــــــــــ اسم ذلك المقهى و ــــــــــــ شربت فيه؟

مـا اسم ذلك المقهى ومـاذا شربت فيه؟

What is the name of that café and what did you drink there?

١ هذه أصوات السيارات.

ــــــــــــ هذه الضجة؟

_____

٢ هو يدرس في مدرسة ثانوية.

ــــــــــــ يعمل والدك؟

_____

٣ أدرس الأدب العربي.

ــــــــــــ تدرس في الجامعة؟

_____

٤ اسمه اسماعيل.

ــــــــــــ اسم صديقك؟

_____

٥ سيارتي زرقاء.

ــــــــــــ لون سيارتك؟

_____

٦ سأذهب مع عائلتي إلى المسبح.

ــــــــــــ ستفعل يوم الجمعة؟

_____

٧ أكلوا الكباب والسلطة.

ــــــــــــ أكلوا في المطعم؟

_____

٨ أنا حزين لأن صديقتي سافرت اليوم.

أنت حزين! ــــــــــــ المشكلة؟

_____

٩ كتبت الوظيفة ثم ذهبت إلى السينما.

_____ فعلت أمس؟

_____

١٠ قرأت قصة مترجمة لزكريا تامر.

_____ قرأت في العطلة؟

_____

_____

Use the appropriate single particles to complete the questions of the following answers. Translate the questions and their answers into English.

EXAMPLE   اسمه "الفردوس" وشربت فيه قهوة. _____ اسم ذلك المقهى و _____ شربت فيه؟

ما اسم ذلك المقهى وماذا شربت فيه؟

What is the name of that café and what did you drink there?

It is called "Al-Firdaws" and I drank coffee in it.

١ سيبدأ الفيلم بعد عشر دقائق.

_____ سيبدأ الفيلم؟

_____

_____

٢ زميل يعمل معي في المكتب.

_____ الذي اتصل بك؟

_____

_____

٣ تعلمت قواعدها في الجامعة أولاً، ثم تعلمت المحادثة في البلدان العربية.

_____ تعلمت اللغة العربية؟

_____

_____

٤ أبي وأمي يسكنان في لندن وأخي يعمل في دبي.

_____ تسكن عائلتك؟

_____

_____

Interrogative pronouns   **69**

٥ تلك السيارة الصغيرة الحمراء.

سيارة سيارتك؟ _____

_____

_____

٦ السكرتيرة.

أخبرك بالقصة؟ _____

_____

_____

٧ بعض الفواكه والخضار.

اشتريت من السوق؟ _____

_____

_____

٨ الأسبوع القادم.

ستزور جدتك؟ _____

_____

_____

٩ في الطابق الثاني.

مكتب المدير؟ _____

_____

_____

١٠ ابن عمي.

صاحب هذا المحل؟ _____

_____

_____

١١ هذا جارنا يغني.

هذا الصوت؟ _____

_____

_____

١٢ صعباً جداً.

كان الامتحان؟ _____

_____

_____

Use the appropriate compound particles to complete the questions of the following answers. Translate the questions and the answers into English.

EXAMPLE

تسكنين؟ _____ مع صديقي.

<u>مع من</u> تسكنين؟

With whom do you live?

With my friend.

١ مع أخي وبعض الأصدقاء.

_____ ستسافر إلى بيروت؟

_____

_____

٢ في جامعة دمشق.

_____ جامعة درست العربية؟

_____

_____

٣ والده مصري ووالدته بريطانية.

_____ صديقك؟

_____

_____

٤ كنت خارج المدينة أزور عائلتي.

_____ لم تحضر المحاضرة اليوم؟

_____

_____

٥ بعشرين ليرة.

_____ اشتريت المجلة الأدبية؟

_____

_____

٦ إلى بغداد.

_____ يذهب هذا القطار؟

_____

_____

٧ حتى نهاية العطلة.

ستبقى في حلب؟ _____

_____

_____

٨ لأن بعض الأصدقاء سيزورونني.

عدت من النادي مبكراً؟ _____

_____

_____

٩ من محل إيراني في السوق القديم.

اشتريت هذه السجادة الجميلة؟ _____

_____

_____

١٠ في الحديقة العامة.

مكان سنلتقي؟ _____

_____

_____

١١ مع مدير الشركة التي سأعمل بها.

كنت تتكلم على الهاتف؟ _____

_____

_____

١٢ إلى المقهى العربي في لندن.

سنذهب بعد الامتحان؟ _____

_____

_____

Yes-no question particles

These types of questions seek yes-no answers. In English, these questions do not have a specific article and they are formed by inverting the word order of the auxiliaries (verb *to be*, verb *to do*, and verb *to have*) and the subject. In Arabic, this question is formed by using the particle هل, and no change occurs in the word order.

We have homework.	عندنا وظيفة.
Do we have homework?	هل عندنا وظيفة؟

Write answers to the following yes-no questions. Translate the yes-no questions into English.

EXAMPLE هل شربت القهوة؟

<u>لا، ما شربت القهوة لأنني كنت أنتظرك/لا لم أشرب القهوة لأنني كنت أنتظرك.</u>

<u>*Did you drink coffee?*</u>

١ هل عندكم امتحان غداً؟

لا، _____

_____

٢ هل أنت موظف في هذه الشركة؟

نعم، _____

_____

٣ هل هذه هي المكتبة التي تفتح يوم السبت؟

نعم، _____

_____

٤ هل رأيتما الفيلم الجديد؟

لا، _____

_____

٥ هل لك خال في أمريكا؟

نعم، _____

_____

٦ هل تريدينني أن أحضر لك شيئاً من السوق؟

لا، _____

_____

٧ هل سنحتاج لكل هذه الحقائب؟

نعم، _____

_____

٨ هل هناك باص إلى شاطئ اللاذقية الجمعة عند منتصف الليل؟

نعم، _____

_____

٩ هل معكم بطاقات للمسرح؟

لا، _____

_____

١٠ هل من الممكن تعلم لغتين في نفس الوقت؟

نعم، _____

_____

١١ هل اتصلت بصديقك الذي تخرج أمس؟

لا، _____

_____

١٢ هل أنت متأكد أنهم سيصلون غداً؟

نعم، _____

_____

EXERCISE
8·5

Translate the following questions into Arabic.

EXAMPLE   Would you like to have lunch with me?

هل تحب أن تتناول الغداء معي؟

Do you know who the new director is? ١

_____

Do you have another car? ٢

_____

Is this the newspaper that published the news? ٢

_____

Is it necessary to translate this question? ٤

_____

Do you know where the University Park is? ٥

_____

Do you have the telephone number of the office? ٦

_____

Do you like Arabic sweets? ٧

_____

Did you send Christmas cards to your friends? ٨

_____

Will your family have a party after you graduate from the university? ٩

_____

Do you have friends in the Arab world? ١٠

_____

Is there a break after this class? ١١

_____

Would you like to have coffee with me? ١٢

_____

Nonhuman third person neutral pronoun

The neutral pronoun "it"

The third person neutral pronoun "it," which is used for nonhumans in English, has no equivalent in Arabic. Instead the subject pronouns for "he" and "she" can be used according to the gender of the noun.

It is a small cow	هـي بقرة صغيرة.
It is a big horse.	هو حصان كبير.
This is my house and it is a beautiful house.	هذا بيتي وهو بيت جميل.
This is my car and it is a new car.	هذه سيارتي وهي سيارة جديدة.

In some expressions the relevant nouns are used in Arabic. Read the following examples in which the relevant added noun is in boldface.

It rained all night.	نزل **المطر** طوال الليل or أمطرت **السماء** طوال الليل.
It gets colder in winter.	**البرد** يشتد في الشتاء or **الطقس** يبرد في الشتاء.
It is warm here.	**الجو** دافئ هنا.
It is very dark in the garden.	**الظلام** شديد في الحديقة.
It is late. We should go home.	تأخر **الوقت**. يجب أن نذهب إلى البيت.

Underline the words that can be replaced by "it" and the phrases that can be changed to include "it" in the following sentences. Translate the sentences into English.

EXAMPLE

<u>الطقس</u> بارد هذا المساء.

It is cold this evening.

١ الحر سيشتد في الصيف.

_____

٢ الثلج ينزل على الجبال.

_____

٣ الوقت مبكر جداً؛ .لا يوجد أحد في المطعم.

_____

٤ هذه فكرة جيدة وهي ذكية أيضاً.

_____

٥ هذا اقتراح عظيم وهو اقتراح جديد أيضاً.

_____

٦ قطتي اسمها فلة وهي قطة جميلة.

_____

٧ كلبي اسمه بوبي وهو كلب ذكي.

_____

٨ الجو غائم اليوم وسينزل المطر طوال الليل.

_____

In some expressions the relevant phrases are used.

It is impossible to finish all the work today.	من المستحيل إنهاء كل العمل اليوم.
It is difficult to memorize the new words.	من الصعب حفظ الكلمات الجديدة.

EXERCISE 9·2

Translate the following sentences into Arabic, substituting the clause that includes the pronoun "it" with the appropriate alternative clause.

EXAMPLE

It is difficult to say goodbye.

من الصعب أن نقول وداعاً.

It is necessary to buy some presents. ١

_____

It is inappropriate to talk about the problem now. ٢

_____

It is possible to study in the library on Saturday. ٣

_____

It is easy to find the house if you have the address. ٤

_____

It is important to prepare for the literature class. ٥

_____

It is clear that he wants to invite her to his party. ٦

_____

It is not important to buy the book because we can borrow it from the library. ٧

_____

EXERCISE 9·3

Translate the following sentences into Arabic, paying attention to the gender that "it" and "its" refer to.

EXAMPLE

My dress is new and its color is blue. I bought it yesterday.

ثوبي جديد ولونه أزرق. اشتريته أمس.

Possessive pronouns:

My car is new and its color is red. ١

_____

My house is white and its door is brown. ٢

_____

The window is open and its glass is very clean. ٣

_____

The book is old and its cover is old too. ٤

_____

Object pronouns:

This is the Arabic magazine. I bought it yesterday. ٥

_____

He gave me the book to read during my vacation. ٦

_____

When he gave me the rose I put it in my book. ٧

_____

This is my favorite film and I have watched it several times. ٨

_____

Other particles and "it":

The coat is beautiful but it is very expensive. ٩

_____

Your garden is full of water and flowers. It looks as if it is a small paradise. ١٠

_____

He spread the rag and sat on it. ١١

_____

I love our house because it is beautiful and spacious. ١٢

_____

Practicing pronouns in context

The following text "A Vacation in Tartous" comprises references to most of the grammatical rules concerning the different kinds of pronouns discussed in Part I.

Read the text carefully paying attention to all the pronouns. Underline these pronouns and the phrases that include pronouns. Categorize them into subject pronouns, possessive pronouns, object pronouns, prepositional pronouns, relative pronouns, interrogative pronouns, and pronouns with other particles. Translate the words and phrases that include these pronouns.

اتصل بي اليوم صديقي أيمن الذي يدرس معي في المدرسة الابتدائية وقال "تبدو سعيداً جداً، لماذا؟"

قلت له: "لأننا مسافرون."

قال: "إلى أين؟"

قلت له "أنا الآن مشغول، سأكتب لك رسالة إلكترونية بعد قليل."

قال: "ومتى ستعودون؟"

قلت: "لا أعرف." بعد دقائق كتبت له هذه الرسالة وأرسلتها بالبريد الإلكتروني:

"أنا سعيد جداً هذا الصباح ... بدأت اليوم عطلة أبي الصيفية ... ستسافر عائلتي إلى مدينة طرطوس غداً لقضاء أسبوعين في المدينة وعلى شاطئها كما نفعل كل سنة. خرج أبي باكراً ليحجز تذاكر سفرنا ... وضعت أمي في حقيبتنا الكبيرة ملابسي وملابس أخوتي الصيفية وثياب سباحتنا وألعابنا المائية و آلات تصويرنا بالإضافة إلى كل ما اشتراه أبي للعطلة.

طرطوس مدينة فينيقية جميلة واسمها الفينيقي "أرادوس." والبحر في تلك المدينة جميل وأمواجه زرقاء.

أنا وأخوتي ووالدي نقضي يومنا عادة في السباحة في البحر وبناء بيوت على رمله، بينما تتناول أمي قهوتها تحت المظلة وهي تنظر إلينا.

كلنا نحب السمك ولذلك نقضي وقت الغداء في المطاعم الجبلية، أو في جزيرة أرواد حيث نتناوله ونحن نستمتع بالطبيعة هناك.

في المساء ننزل إلى المدينة ونتمشى في شوارعها أو نزور أقاربنا وكل من يدعونا من أصدقاء والدي. ونخرج معهم أحيانا إلى المطاعم والمقاهي."

First translate the following text "My Friend" into Arabic. Then rewrite the whole text five times changing the masculine third person (i.e, "student") to:

Feminine third person singular هي

Masculine third person dual هما

Feminine third person dual هما

Masculine third person plural هم

Feminine third person plural هن

This is the student whom I met last month. We became friends because he is very kind and is studying Arabic like me at the University of Damascus. He likes the Arabic language and he speaks it fluently with his Arab friends. I traveled with him last week to Aleppo and Baalbek and I visited him yesterday at his house, which is located in the old city. He introduced me to his friend, who lives near him and studies Arabic as well.

_____

_____

_____

_____

_____

_____

_____

_____

Feminine third person singular هي:

_____

_____

_____

_____

_____

_____

_____

Masculine third person dual هما:

_____

_____

_____

_____

_____

_____

_____

Feminine third person dual هـمـا:

_____
_____
_____
_____
_____
_____
_____

Masculine third person plural هـم:

_____
_____
_____
_____
_____
_____
_____

Feminine third person plural هـن:

_____
_____
_____
_____
_____
_____
_____

PREPOSITIONS

Arabic prepositions can be divided into two types according to their forms: attached prepositions and separate prepositions. The second type includes a group termed "**dharf**" by Arab grammarians. Strictly speaking, **dharf** words are nouns in the accusative. However, they function similarly to prepositions and so are often listed as a subcategory of prepositions in references for learners of Arabic as a foreign language.

Prepositions are followed by genitive nouns or by attached pronouns. The noun that follows a preposition and is governed by it is called **ism majrūr**. The prepositional phrase, which consists of a preposition and a genitive noun or a pronoun, is called **jar wa majrūr**.

Inseparable prepositions

Introduction to inseparable prepositions

Inseparable prepositions are also called attached prepositions. This group of prepositions includes four prepositions. Each one of these prepositions consists of one letter that cannot stand alone, it is always attached to the next word.

The preposition بـ

This preposition is used to indicate "in," "by," or "with."

We sat on a bench in the garden.	جلسنا على مقعد بالحديقة.
I write with a pen.	أكتب بالقلم.
I travel by plane.	أسافر بالطائرة.
How much is one kilogram of oranges?	بكم كيلو البرتقال؟
It is forty pounds.	بأربعين ليرة.

The preposition تـ

This preposition is used for giving an oath or swearing. It usually occurs at the beginning of the sentence and is followed by the word *Allah*. It is not preceded by the verb *to swear*, as in the common oath and swear phrase أقسم بالله (*I swear to God*). تالله is unlikely to stand alone as such; usually, it is followed by a verbal phrase.

I swear to God that I will say the truth.	تالله لأقول الحق.

The preposition كـ

This preposition is used to indicate "as" or "like."

We do not accept a solution as such/like this.	لا نقبل حلاً كهذا.
The baby is like an angel.	الطفل كالملاك.

The preposition لـ

This preposition indicates "to," "for," "because of," "in order to," or "until."

The student went to school.	ذهب التلميذ للمدرسة.
I bought a pot for cooking.	اشتريت وعاء للطبخ.
I will take the bus in order to arrive early.	سآخذ الباص للوصول مبكراً.
We stayed up until morning.	سهرنا للصبح.

EXERCISE
11·1

Fill in the following spaces with the correct preposition. Translate the sentences into English.

EXAMPLE   ذهبت إلى المكتبة لقراءة الكتاب. <u>I went to the library to read the book.</u>

١ وضع النقود ـــــــــــــــ جيبه.

_____

٢ كيف يمكنك أن تصادق شخصاً ـــــــــــــــ هذا!

_____

٣ سافر ـــــــــــــــ القطار من القاهرة لأسوان.

_____

٤ ذهبنا ـــــــــــــــ لمقهى يوم الجمعة.

_____

٥ ذهبا ـــــــــــــــ السينما ـــــــــــــــ مشاهدة الفيلم.

_____

٦ كلمته من المطار ـــــــــــــــ هاتفها الجوال.

_____

٧ نمنا يوم الأحد ـــــــــــــــ الساعة العاشرة.

_____

٨ ـــــــــــــــ كم اشتريت خاتمك الذهبي؟

_____

٩ ـــــــــــــــ الله لأنجح في الامتحان.

_____

١٠ الفتاة جميلة ـــــــــــــــ الوردة.

_____

١١.هو قوي ـــــــــــــــ النمر.

_____

١٢ اشتريت حقيبة جديدة ـــــــــــــــ ألف ليرة.

_____

١٣ وضع صورتها ـــــــــــــــ إطار.

_____

١٤ هذا الرجل يمشي ـــــــــــــــ راعي البقر.

_____

١٥ أخبرت أصدقائي _____ _____ الهاتف.

_____

١٦ قدم الوظيفة _____ _____ لأستاذ.

_____

١٧ يركض _____ _____ الحصان.

_____

١٨ _____ الله لآخذ حقي.

_____

١٩ مشيت _____ _____ بيت أصدقائي.

_____

٢٠ أفضل السفر _____ _____ القطار على السفر بالباص.

_____

٢١ الغرفة باردة _____ الثلاجة.

_____

٢٢ بقيت _____ المساء في البيت.

_____

٢٣ سأذهب إلى مكتبة الجامعة _____ _____ كتابة البحث.

_____

٢٤ الصديق الوفي _____ الأخ.

_____

٢٥ ذهب _____ مكتبه بالسيارة.

_____

Using inseparable prepositions with attached pronouns

Of the four inseparable prepositions, only بـ and لـ can be used with attached pronouns.

I trust him.	أثق به.
What is the matter with you?	مابك؟
They welcomed us.	رحبوا بنا.
She told you that.	قالت لكَ ذلك.
I sent them many books.	أرسلت لهم عدة كتب.

The preposition بـ is associated with certain verbs.

to keep, to maintain	احتفظ بـ
to take for granted	استهان ب
to confess, to recognize	اعترف بـ
to have a strong belief in	اعتقد بـ
to admire	أعجب بـ
to follow as a model or an example, to be guided by	اقتدى بـ
to be convinced of	اقتنع بـ
to be committed to	التزم بـ
to join	التحق بـ
to believe in	آمن بـ
to dream of	حلم بـ
to welcome	رحب بـ
to be content with	رضي بـ
to have a knowledge of, to be informed about, to know about	علم بـ
to lose faith in	كفر بـ
to pass by, to step by	مر بـ
to trust, to have a trust in	وثق بـ
to take care of, to take interest in	اهتم بـ

EXERCISE

11·2

Study the verbs that are associated with the preposition بـ and fill in the following spaces by combining them with the relevant attached pronouns as in the example.

EXAMPLE   ما اسم الجامعة التي يريد أن يلتحق بها؟

١ هذا هو القلم الذي كتبت _____ الرسالة.

٢ استقبل الوزير الضيوف ورحب _____ .

٣ شرحت لهما الموضوع وأقنعتهما _____ .

٤ يحترم الحب ويؤمن _____ .

٥ ويحترم الصداقة، ولكنه لا يؤمن _____ .

٦ لا يحبك، ولكنه معجب ــــــــــــــــــــــــــ.

٧ سأريك بعض صور طفولتي التي أحتفظ ــــــــــــــــــــــــــ.

٨ وثقت ــــــــــــــــــــــــــ، وحكت لهن عن مشكلتها.

٩ هم معجبون بوالديهم، ويحاولون أن يقتدوا ــــــــــــــــــــــــــ.

١٠ قدموا وعوداً كثيرة لكنهم لم يلتزموا ــــــــــــــــــــــــــ.

١١ مروا ــــــــــــــــــــــــــ وخذوني معكم إذا قررتم الخروج.

١٢ ما ــــــــــــــــــــــــــ؟ لقد تغيروا كثيراً.

١٣ طرح عليها حلاً لكنها لم ترض ــــــــــــــــــــــــــ.

١٤ يحبان أطفالهما كثيراً ويهتمان ــــــــــــــــــــــــــ.

١٥ هل تذكرون عندما التقيت ــــــــــــــــــــــــــ لأول مرة في المكتبة.

١٦ يحب السفر إلى البلدان البعيدة التي يحلم ــــــــــــــــــــــــــ أحياناً.

١٧ هذا هو المقهى الذي تعارفنا ــــــــــــــــــــــــــ.

١٨ نحن أقوياء فلا تستهينوا ــــــــــــــــــــــــــ.

١٩ تذكرت كل التجارب التي مررت ــــــــــــــــــــــــــ خلال هذه السنوات.

٢٠ سأرسل في العيد رسائل لأساتذتي الذين أحبهم، أو سأتصل ــــــــــــــــــــــــــ.

Using the preposition ـل with direct objects

ـل usually follows certain verbs that take an indirect object.

to send to	أرسل لـ
to express to	عبّر لـ
to say to	قال لـ
to give to, to present to	قدم لـ
to occur to	خطر لـ

In addition, it follows certain verbs including these:

to need	احتاج لـ
to miss	اشتاق لـ
to be forced to, to find it necessary to	اضطر لـ
to forgive	غفر لـ

EXERCISE
11·3

Study the verbs that are associated with the preposition لـ and fill in the following spaces by combining them with the relevant attached pronouns as in the example. Translate the new sentences into English.

EXAMPLE   أعدت الكتاب _____ هم. أُعدت الكتاب لهم.

I returned the book to them.

١ تكلمت معه بالعربية فلم يفهموا ما قالته _____.

_____

٢ توفي والدهن وترك _____ مالاً كثيراً.

_____

٣ لن أطلب منكم المساعدة إلا إذا احتجت _____.

_____

٤ كنت أمشي في الشارع حين ظهر _____ فجأة.

_____

٥ هؤلاء هم أصدقاؤك المخلصون فاغفر _____ إذا أخطؤوا أحياناً.

_____

٦ اشتاق _____ كثيراً يا أحبابي.

_____

٧ انظر إلى الكاميرا وابتسم _____.

_____

٨ اعترفت _____ أنها وقعت في حب زميلها.

_____

٩ أرسل _____ صور قريتك الجميلة.

_____

١٠ سنقدم _____ اقتراحاً عظيماً عندما نلقاكما.

_____

١١ تركت _____ على طاولة المطبخ البقلاوة التي تحبها.

_____

١٢ لا يحب استعمال السيارة إلا إذا اضطر _____.

_____

١٣ قابلنا وعبر _____ عن قلقه من الموضوع.

_____

١٤ لمح _____ عن خطته عدة مرات عندما التقاهما.

_____

١٥ عندما سيلقاها سيهمس _____ بكلمات الحب.

_____

١٦ سمعنا أنك ستعزف على العود في المقهى فجئنا لنستمع _____ .

_____

١٧ لم أسمع أخباركن منذ زمن. ماذا حدث _____ يا صديقاتي.

_____

١٨ سأزورهم غدا لأنني اشتقت _____ كثيراً.

_____

١٩ أخبروني كل ما الذي حدث _____ مذ سافرتم.

_____

٢٠ عندما مر التاكسي لوح _____ فتوقفت.

_____

٢١ سيعطي حبيبته الهدايا التي اشتراها _____ .

_____

Separate prepositions

Introduction to separate prepositions

Separate prepositions consist of more than one letter and they can stand alone, independent from the following noun. However, they can be combined with attachable pronouns. This group includes two categories:

1. Particles (they are also called short prepositions and in Arabic they are called **hurūf al-jarr**, pl. for **harf jarr**)

2. **Dharf**-prepositions (they are also called nouns in the accusative)

Both particle-prepositions (**hurūf al-jarr**) and **dharf**-prepositions can be followed by a noun in the genitive. When the noun follows a **harf jarr**, it is called **ism majrūr**, whereas the genitive noun after the **dharf** is called **idafa**. The **idafa** and **ism majrūr** are both genitive.

Particle prepositions

Particle prepositions include:

to, until إلى

| We went to the exhibition. | ذهبنا إلى المعرض. |

| We looked at the paintings. | نظرنا إلى اللوحات. |

| We stayed up until dawn. | سهرنا إلى الفجر. |

until, up to, as far as, to حتى

| We walked together to the end of the street. | مشينا معاً حتى نهاية الشارع. |

| We sat in the café until midnight. | جلسنا في المقهى حتى منتصف الليل. |

without دون/من دون

| We will drink coffee without sugar. | سنتناول القهوة دون/من دون سكر. |

on, over, above على

| Books are on the shelves. | الكتب على الرفوف. |

from, about, concerning عن

His house is very far from the university.

بيته بعيد جدًا عن الجامعة.

We talked about the past.

تكلمنا عن الماضي.

in في

We stayed in the club until the evening.

بقينا في النادي حتى المساء.

with, at, upon لدي، لدى

Do you have a pen with you?

هل لديك قلم؟

I welcomed him upon his arrival at the station.

استقبلته لدى وصوله إلى المحطة.

I won't go to the cinema because I have a lot of work.

لن أذهب إلى السينما لأن لدي عمل كثير.

with مع

I spent the night yesterday with some friends.

سهرت البارحة مع بعض الأصدقاء.

from, of من

I bought fruit from the market.

اشتريت فواكه من السوق.

EXERCISE
12·1

Fill in the following spaces using the appropriate particle prepositions.

EXAMPLE   سنذهب إلى المطعم. (We will go to the restaurant.)

١ هو مختلف _____ بقية أصدقائه.

٢ في الصباح يشرب الإنكليز عادة الشاي _____ الحليب أما الفرنسيون فيشربون القهوة _____ حليب.

٣ نسي القاموس _____ المكتبة.

٤ اشتريت _____ السوق القديم ركوة قهوة.

٥ استلقى _____ السرير وأخذ يفكر.

٦ مشينا معاً _____ المحطة.

٧ أدرس _____ البيت أحياناً، ولكنني أفضل الدراسة _____ المكتبة.

٨ عاد _____ العمل مبكراً اليوم.

٩ سيسافر غداً _____ السعودية.

١٠ قضيت عيد الميلاد _____ أسرتي.

١١ وضع الكتاب _____ الرف.

١٢ تكلم في محاضرته _____ الحقوق المدنية.

١٣ هل _____ المدير أية مواعيد اليوم؟

١٤ بيته يقع _____ وسط المدينة.

١٥ حضرت فيلماً وثائقياً _____ الحرب العالمية الأولى.

١٦ شربنا قهوة _____ المقهى العربي.

١٧ وضعنا الصحون _____ طاولة الطعام.

١٨ انتظرناهم _____ المساء لكنهم لم يأتوا.

١٩ سيذهبان _____ المسرح يوم الأحد.

٢٠ لن يأتي إلى الحفلة _____ صديقته.

Particle prepositions with suffixes

Apart from حتى, all the listed separate prepositions can be followed by attachable pronouns, that is, suffixes. And with the exception of إلى and على, no changes occur to the ending of the preposition.

He visited us several times with his wife and twice without her.	زارنا عدة مرات مع زوجته ومرتين من دونها.
He loves his work and he speaks a lot about it.	يحب عمله ويتكلم عنه كثيراً.
I opened the book and found the ticket in it.	فتحت الكتاب فوجدت البطاقة فيه.
This is the shop where she buys her clothes.	هذا هو المحل الذي تشتري منه ملابسها.
I met my cousin on the street so I walked home with him.	صادفت ابن عمي في الطريق فتمشيت معه إلى البيت.
They (pl. f.) did not attend the party because they have an exam tomorrow.	لم يحضرن الحفلة لأن لديهن امتحانا غداً.

EXERCISE
12·2

Fill in the following spaces by combining the appropriate prepositions with relevant suffixes.

EXAMPLE هذه هي الحديقة التي جلسنا <u>فيها</u>. (This is the park where we sat.)

١ ما اسم الجامعة التي تخرج _____ ابنك؟

٢ ذهب _____ إلى المطار.

٣ هذه هي الغرفة التي أسكن _____.

٤ منذ عودته من رحلة القاهرة لم يتوقف عن الحديث _____.

٥ تعرفت في الرباط على أصدقاء جدد وسافرت _____ إلى مراكش.

٦ سأذهب _____ إذا كنتم لا تريدون الذهاب معي إلى الحفلة.

٧ _____ اختبار في اللغة العربية غداً.

٨ اتصلنا بأسرتك وسألناها _____ .

٩ أعجب باللوحة والألوان التي استخدمت _____ .

١٠ سأقضي هذا المساء في المكتب لأن _____ عمل كثير.

١١ أعادوا لي المجلات التي أخذوها _____ .

١٢ يتمنى أن يزور البيت الذي ولد _____ .

١٣ غضب _____ بسبب تصرفكما الغريب.

١٤ هذا هو الكتاب الذي حدثتك _____ .

١٥ هذا هو المدير الذي لا أحب أن أعمل _____ .

١٦ أقنعته بزيارة المدينة التي تعيش _____ .

١٧ لن أذهب _____ إلى أي مكان أبداً.

١٨ أرسلت بطاقات بريدية لأصدقائي الذين درست _____ في الجامعة.

١٩ أعادوا لنا الكتب التي أخذوها _____ .

٢٠ اشترى حقيبة ووضع كتبه _____ .

٢١ زاروا أصدقاءنا وسألوهم _____ .

Combining إلى and على with suffixes

When إلى and على are followed by a suffix, the **alif maqsura** ى turns into a **ya'** ي. The two **ya's** of the first person singular are joined, and the **shadda** is placed on the **ya'**.

أنا: عليّ	أنا: إليّ
نحن: علينا	نحن: إلينا
أنتَ: عليكَ	أنتَ: إليكَ
أنتِ: عليك	أنتِ: إليكِ
أنتما: عليكما	أنتما: إليكما
أنتم: عليكم	أنتم: إليكم
أنتن: عليكن	أنتن: إليكن
هو: عليه	هو: إليه
هي: عليها	هي: إليها
هما: عليهما	هما: إليهما
هم: عليك	هم: إليكم
هن: عليهن	هن: إليهن

EXERCISE
12·3

Complete the following sentences by changing the subject pronouns in parentheses into attached pronouns and then combining them with the particle prepositions. Translate your answers into English.

EXAMPLE

(في، هي) هذه هي الكلية التي يدِّرس ــــــــــــــــــــــ .

هذه هي الكلية التي يدِّرس فيها.

This is the college where he teaches.

١ (إلى، أنا) نظر ــــــــــــــــــــــ و لم يقل شيئاً.

ـــ

٢ (على، هو) انكسر الرف لأننا وضعنا القواميس الضخمة ــــــــــــــــــــــ .

ـــ

٣ (على، هما) شعرت بالقلق ــــــــــــــــــــــ .

ـــ

٤ (إلى، هي) يتذكر كل الأماكن التي ذهب ــــــــــــــــــــــ في القاهرة.

ـــ

٥ (على أنتن) السلام ــــــــــــــــــــــ أيتها الصديقات.

ـــ

٦ (إلى، هما) أرسلت ــــــــــــــــــــــ رسالة منذ شهر.

ـــ

٧ (على، أنا) يجب ــــــــــــــــــــــ الذهاب إلى المكتبة.

ـــ

٨ (إلى، نحن) أرسلوا ــــــــــــــــــــــ بعض الهدايا.

ـــ

٩ (على، أنتم) ــــــــــــــــــــــ أن تدرسوا للامتحان.

ـــ

١٠ (إلى، نحن)جاء ــــــــــــــــــــــ من بعيد.

ـــ

١١ (إلى، أنت) سيقدم ــــــــــــــــــــــ هدية.

ـــ

١٢ (على، هم) تعرفت ــــــــــــــــــــــ في دمشق.

ـــ

١٣ (إلى، أنت) انظر _____ عندما أتحدث إليك.

_____

١٤ (إلى، هو) أعادت _____ كل الهدايا والرسائل.

_____

١٥ (على، هو) طلب كرسياً ليجلس _____.

_____

١٦ (إلى، هم) أرسلت _____ عدة رسائل.

_____

١٧ (على، أنت) أنت صديقي وأنا اعتمد _____.

_____

١٨ (على، هي) حدثتهم عن الوظيفة التي حصلت _____.

_____

١٩ (إلى، هن) قدم _____ نصيحة.

_____

٢٠ (إلى، أنتن) جئنا _____ بأخبار سعيدة.

_____

◆·13·◆ Dharf

Introduction to dharf

Dharf words are "un-nunated" nouns in the accusative and they can be categorized into **dharf zaman** (*adverb of time*) and **dharf makan** (*adverb of place*). However, some of the adverbs can refer to both time and place.

during	أثناء
in front of, before, opposite, ahead of	أمام
after (of time or rank or place)	بعد
between	بين
opposite, facing	مقابل
under, below (of place or rank)	تحت
about, around	حول
when, at (the time of)	حين/عند
outside	خارج
through, during	خلال
behind	خلف
inside	داخل
under, on the side of	دون
towards, in the direction of	نحو
towards	صوب،اتجاه، تجاه
throughout	طوال
across	عبر
with, at	عند
instead of, in place of	عوض
on, over, above (of place and rank)	فوق
before	قبل
before (indicates location)	قدام
facing, opposite, equivalent	مقابل
since	منذ
behind, on the far side of	وراء
in the middle of, midst of, amid, between	وسط
opposite, face to face with, vis-à-vis, in front of	قبالة

Classical and literary adverbs

These adverbs are more common in classical texts. They still occur in high-discourse texts, including literary texts. As the preceding list shows, all of them have synonyms in modern standard Arabic.

after	عقب
opposite	تلقاء
opposite	حذاء
after	غب
after	تلو
after	إثر
since	مذ

Although مذ can be found in both literary and modern standard Arabic, it is more literary and classical.

EXERCISE 13·1

*Fill in the spaces with the appropriate **dharf**. Translate the completed sentences into English.*

EXAMPLE   ذهبنا مباشرة بعد الحفلة. *We went directly after the party.*

١ كنت أطبخ العشاء ــــــــــــــــــــــ دخولك.

_____

٢ تجمع الطلاب ــــــــــــــــــــــ القاعة.

_____

٣ لدي اجتماع مهم الآن. سأراك ــــــــــــــــــــــ ساعة.

_____

٤ نام ــــــــــــــــــــــ الفيلم.

_____

٥ وقف الطفل ــــــــــــــــــــــ أمه.

_____

٦ أخفى شعوره ــــــــــــــــــــــ صديقته.

_____

٧. من الرجل الواقف ــــــــــــــــــــــ المدير والسكرتيرة؟

_____

٨ أوقف سيارته ــــــــــــــــــــــ باب المكتب.

_____

٩ القطة نائمة ــــــــــــــــــــــ السرير.

_____

١٠ جلسنا معاً _____ الطاولة.

_____

١١ سأكتب الرسالة _____ الأسبوع القادم.

_____

١٢ انتظر الطالب الأستاذ _____ المكتب.

_____

١٣ عند التقييم السنوي وضعه المدير في مرتبة _____ مراتب زملائه في العمل.

_____

١٤ مشينا بسرعة _____ المكتبة.

_____

١٥ التفت _____ البحر.

_____

١٦ نام _____ المحاضرة.

_____

١٧ ركضنا تحت المطر _____ الشارع.

_____

١٨ اجتمع الناس _____ بوابة المعرض.

_____

١٩ وضعنا الطاولة _____ الغرفة.

_____

٢٠ مشت القطة _____ السطح.

_____

٢١ نام ساعة _____ الغداء.

_____

٢٢ أوقف السيارة _____ البيت.

_____

٢٣ انتظرها _____ الباب.

_____

٢٤ انتظرناهم في المقهى _____ الانتظار في الشارع.

_____

٢٥ اجتمع الناس _____ المعرض.

_____

Dharf and attached pronouns

The **dharf** words/adverbs listed here can be followed by attached pronouns instead of nouns:

أثناء،بعد، بين، تجاه، تحت، حول، حين، خارج، خلال، خلف، داخل، دون، صوب، عبر،
عند، فوق، قبالة، قبل، قدام، مقابل، وسط، أمام، وراء، نحو

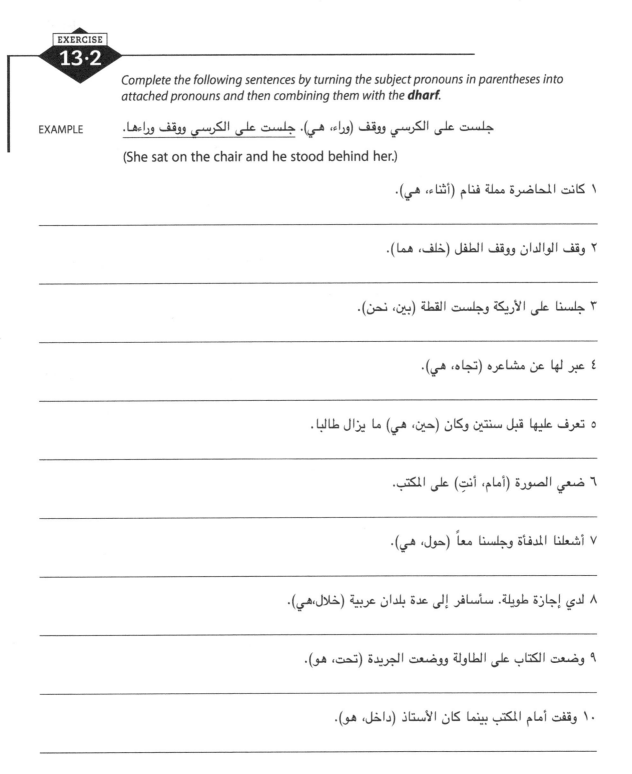

EXERCISE
13·2

*Complete the following sentences by turning the subject pronouns in parentheses into attached pronouns and then combining them with the **dharf**.*

EXAMPLE

جلست على الكرسي ووقف (وراء، هي). <u>جلست على الكرسي ووقف وراءها.</u>

(She sat on the chair and he stood behind her.)

١ كانت المحاضرة مملة فنام (أثناء، هي).

_____

٢ وقف الوالدان ووقف الطفل (خلف، هما).

_____

٣ جلسنا على الأريكة وجلست القطة (بين، نحن).

_____

٤ عبر لها عن مشاعره (تجاه، هي).

_____

٥ تعرف عليها قبل سنتين وكان (حين، هي) ما يزال طالبا.

_____

٦ ضعي الصورة (أمام، أنتِ) على المكتب.

_____

٧ أشعلنا المدفأة وجلسنا معاً (حول، هي).

_____

٨ لدي إجازة طويلة. سأسافر إلى عدة بلدان عربية (خلال،هي).

_____

٩ وضعت الكتاب على الطاولة ووضعت الجريدة (تحت، هو).

_____

١٠ وقفت أمام المكتب بينما كان الأستاذ (داخل، هو).

_____

١١ أنتما متكبران وتشعران أن كل الناس (دون، أنتما) في الأهمية.

_____

١٢ رأينا صديقنا فمشينا (نحو، هو).

_____

١٣ أغلقت السكرتيرة القاعة فتجمع الطلاب (خارج، هي).

_____

١٤ خرجت من الاجتماع (بعد، أنتن) بدقيقة.

_____

١٥ دخلنا الحديقة ومشينا (عبر، هي).

_____

١٦ هذا هو بيتنا، و(مقابل، هو) بيت جدي.

_____

١٧ كليتنا في آخر الشارع و(قبالة، هي) تقع المكتبة.

_____

١٨ رأوا الطائرات تحلق (فوق، هم).

_____

١٩ ذهبوا إلى الحفلة (قبل، هن) بساعة.

_____

٢٠ وقف (قدام، نحن) وقرأ القصيدة.

_____

٢١ أقامت الجدة حفلة واجتمعت العائلة (عند، هي).

_____

٢٢ وضعنا الصحون على الطاولة ووضعنا المزهرية في (وسط، هي).

_____

٢٣ التفت (صوب، ي) حين سمع صوتي.

_____

Dharf and verbal phrases

Five **dharf** prepositions can be followed by verbal phrases. These prepositions are:

بعد، حيث، حين، قبل، منذ/مذ

بعد can be followed by "أن" and a past tense verb or a present tense verb. قبل can be followed by "أن" and a present tense verb. حين, حيث, and منذ/مذ can be followed by verbs directly.

I had a cup of coffee after I had lunch.	تناولت القهوة بعد أن تناولت الغداء.
I will have a cup of coffee after I have lunch.	سأتناول القهوة بعد أن أتناول الغداء.
He studied in the library before he went to the lecture.	درس في المكتبة قبل أن يذهب إلى المحاضرة.
He parked his car where parking is allowed.	أوقف سيارته حيث يسمح بالوقوف.
He parked his car where cars are usually parked.	أوقف سيارته حيث تقف السيارات عادة.
The students stood up when the teacher entered the classroom.	وقف الطلاب حين دخل الأستاذ إلى الصف.
I have not seen him since we attended the party together last time.	لم أره منذ حضرنا الحفلة معا آخر مرة.

However, these verbal sentences can be turned into nominal sentences by deriving the **masdar** (*the verbal noun*) of the verb.

I had coffee after having lunch.	تناولت القهوة بعد تناول الغداء.
I will have coffee after having lunch.	سأتناول القهوة بعد تناول الغداء.
He studied at the library before going to the lecture.	درس في المكتبة قبل الذهاب إلى المحاضرة.
He parked his car where parking is allowed.	أوقف سيارته حيث الوقوف مسموح.
The students stood up at the teacher's entrance to the class	وقف الطلاب حين دخول الأستاذ إلى الصف.
I didn't see him since the last time we attended the party together.	لم أره منذ حضورنا الحفلة معا آخر مرة.

Fill in the following spaces with the appropriate adverb and the necessary article and then turn the verbal phrase into a nominal phrase.

EXAMPLE   سنتناول الغداء <u>قبل أن نذهب</u> إلى السوق. (.We will have lunch before we go to the market)

سنتناول الغداء <u>قبل الذهاب إلى السوق</u>. (.We will have lunch before going to the market)

١ ذهب إلى مكتب البريد ـــــــــــــــــــــــــــ كتب الرسالة.

_____

٢ شعرت الفتاة بالفرح ـــــــــــــــــــــــــــ رأت صديقها.

_____

٣ سأزور صديقي ـــــــــــــــــــــــــــ أتصل به.

_____

٤ لم نركم ـــــــــــــــــــــــــــ زرناكم آخر مرة.

_____

٥ سأقرأ الكتاب ـــــــــــــــــــــــــــ أسافر.

_____

٦ خرجوا من المكتبة ـــــــــــــــــــــــــــ قرأوا كتبهم.

_____

٧ لم أتغيب عن أي محاضرة ـــــــــــــــــــــــــــ عدت من سفري.

_____

٨ بدأت حياتي ـــــــــــــــــــــــــــ تعرفت عليك.

_____

٩ سنذهب إلى المقهى ـــــــــــــــــــــــــــ نشاهد الفيلم.

_____

١٠ لم آخذ إجازة ـــــــــــــــــــــــــــ بدأت العمل هنا.

_____

١١ سأذهب إلى السوق ـــــــــــــــــــــــــــ أنتهي من العمل.

_____

١٢ هل أنهيتِ الكتاب ـــــــــــــــــــــــــــ تنامي؟

_____

Combining **dharf** with prepositions

A preposition can be followed by a **dharf**. The combination sometimes indicates a new or additional meaning. The combination can be followed by either a noun or an attached pronoun. When the **dharf** is followed by a noun, this noun will be called an **idafa** and it is put in the genitive. Some of the common combinations are as follows:

without	بدون
without	من دون
after	من بعدِ
from between them, from the midst of	من بين
from under, from underneath	من تحت
in front of (for verbs of movement)	من أمام
to the front, forward	إلى الأمام
on the basis of, by means of	من خلال
in such a manner that, so as to, so that	بحيث
whence	من حيث
whither	إلى حيث
backward	إلى الوراء، إلى الخلف
in the rear, at the back	في الخلف
from behind	من الخلف
from over, down from	من على
from with	من عند
from over, from above	من فوق
before	من قبلِ
after, in the wake of, in the aftermath of	في أعقاب
as an equivalent	بالمقابل، في مقابل
for nothing, gratis	بدون مقابل

Some of these combinations can be used with both nominal and verbal sentences.

next to, near بجانب

The house is near the market.	البيت بجانب السوق.
He sat next to me.	جلس بجانبي.
He walked next to me.	مشى بجانبي.

close to, near, next to بجوار

The house is close to the university.
البيت بجوار الجامعة.

He sat next to his relatives.
جلس بجوار أقاربه.

He lives near his relatives.
يسكن بجوار أقاربه.

However, some of them are exclusively used with verbs of actions.

١ من أمام

مر من أمام بيتها.

٢ من بين

ظهر فجأة كلب من بين الأشجار.

٣ من تحت

مروا من تحت العلم.

٤ من خلال

رأيته من خلال زجاج النافذة.

٥ من خلف

ناديته من خلف الباب.

٦ من وراء

ناديته من وراء الباب.

EXERCISE 13·4

Fill in the following spaces with adverbs combined with prepositions to match the English translation.

EXAMPLE   They came out from under the bridge. خرجوا <u>من تحت</u> الجسر.

١ جلست ــــــــــــــــ أثناء المحاضرة. She sat beside him during the lecture.

٢ ساعدته في كتابة الوظيفة، وهو ــــــــــــــــ أصلح لها دراجتها.
She helped him in writing the homework and, in return, he repaired her bicycle.

٣ نشرب الشاي ــــــــــــــــ حليب. We drink tea without milk.

٤ خرج ــــــــــــــــ الطلاب واحد وألقى خطاباً.
One student emerged from amongst the students and delivered a speech.

٥ خرج الرجل ــــــــــــــــ الخيمة. A man emerged from under the tent.

٦ جلس في المقعد الأمامي وجلسنا ــــــــــــــــ.
He sat in the front seat, and we sat in the back.

٧ عبر ــــــــــــــــ بصمت. He crossed in front of us silently.

٨ مشى خطوتين ــــــــــــــــ وخطوة ــــــــــــــــ.
He walked two steps forward and one step backward.

٩ وقع الفنجان ـــــــــــــــــــــ الطاولة. The cup fell down from the table.

١٠ قفز ـــــــــــــــــــــ السور. He jumped over the fence.

١١ هو يقدم خدمات كثيرة لجيرانه ـــــــــــــــــــــ .

He provides plenteous services to his neighbors for free.

١٢ صاحب المكتبة صديقي ولهذا أشتري كتبي ـــــــــــــــــــــ .

The bookshop owner is my friend and that's why I buy my books from him.

١٣ ـــــــــــــــــــــ الحرب صنعت أفلام كثيرة لتبرير ما حدث.

In the aftermath of war, many films were made to justify what happened.

١٤ جلست في آخر صف ـــــــــــــــــــــ أراه ولا يراني.

I sat in the last row so I can see him and he cannot see me.

Dharf prepositions that function as adverbs

Sometimes a **dharf** can stand alone without an **idafa**, in which case it is "un-nunated" nominative and it functions like the English adverb.

afterwards	من بعدُ
earlier, previously	من قبلِ
not yet	ما ... بعد

Adverbs constitute part of set phrases, terms, and idioms. They can sometimes have a metaphoric meaning.

at your disposal, at your disposition	تحت تصرفك
irrelevant	خارج عن الموضوع
out of his control	خارج عن إرادته
undoubtedly	دون شك
around the world	حول العالم
trans-continental	عبر القارات
above his capability	فوق طاقته
in the best way possible	بأفضل طريقة
in principle	من حيث المبدأ
on the basis of, by means of, through	من خلال
ahead of	أمام
in front of my eyes	أمام عيني

Match the phrases in list A with the appropriate complement in list B.

B	A
فأنا أضع سيارتي تحت تصرفك	هذه فكرة جيدة
فالموضوع خارج تماما عن إرادتي	إذا لم يكن عندك سيارة
ويحب المساعدة وهو سيساعدك دون شك	لا أستطيع مساعدتكم أبدا
وكتاباته معروفة حول العالم كله	لا أعرف هذا الطالب
ولكنها خارجة عن الموضوع	أدونيس كاتب مشهور
وسوف تساعدكن على قدر طاقتها	نحن متأكدون أنه شخص طيب
ولم أقابله من قبل	هي تتفهم مشكلتكن
لأننا نختلف معهم من حيث المبدأ	أنا أختلف معك على بعض التفاصيل
والمستقبل كله أمامك	لا يمكن أن نتفق معهم أبدا
ولكني أتفق معك من حيث المبدأ	هي تستخدم الإنترنت كثيرا
وقد تعرفت على صديقها من خلال إحدى مواقع الإنترنت	اكتشفوا كل أسرارهن
كان يلعب في الغرفة وأوقعها عن الطاولة أمام عيني	تفاءل فمازلت شابا
انس تلك التجربة وضع الماضي كله وراءك	عليكما أن تستعدا جيدا
لأن أمامكما سنة من العمل الجاد	أخوك الصغير هو الذي كسر المزهرية
من خلال قراءتهم لرسائلهن	لا تلتفت إلى الوراء

Different functions of prepositional phrases

·14·

In Arabic, prepositional phrases can have different grammatical functions. The categories discussed in this chapter represent the major areas and the most common patterns.

Prepositional phrases as adverbial phrases

Some adverbs in English are translated into Arabic by using prepositional phrases:

gently	بلطف
harshly	بقسوة
rudely	بوقاحة
politely	بتهذيب
softly	برقة
respectfully	باحترام
patiently	بصبر
quickly	بسرعة
in the best conditions, in the best state	في أحسن حال
immediately	في الحال
as well as one could possibly wish, in excellent state	على ما يرام
in the hope (that)	على أمل
in the same manner, the way	على منوال
confident, certain, sure	على ثقة
in poverty, in destitution, in annoyance	في ضيق
in happiness	في سعادة
in misery	في بؤس
in bliss	في هناء
in particular, particularly	بصورة خاصة، بصفة خاصة، بشكل خاص
in general, generally	بصورة عامة، بصفة عامة، بشكل عام

EXERCISE
14·1

Underline all adverbs that are expressed by using prepositional phrases in the following sentences. Translate the sentences into English.

EXAMPLE يتكلم <u>بثقة</u>. _He speaks confidently._

١ يتعامل مع جيرانه باحترام.

_____

٢ انتظروهم في المحطة بصبر.

_____

٣ كان متأخراً ولذلك مشى بسرعة.

_____

٤ عاشوا في شقاء إلى أن وجد والدهم عملاً.

_____

٥ هم على ما يرام ويرسلون تحياتهم.

_____

٦ قال لها وداعاً على أمل اللقاء ثانية.

_____

٧ كتب الجواب على منوال السؤال.

_____

٨ أنا على ثقة أنهم سيدرسون جيداً للامتحان.

_____

٩ غادرت البيت هذا الصباح على عجل.

_____

١٠ مشى على مهل يفكر في مستقبله.

_____

١١ تعزف على البيانو وتغني بطريقة جميلة.

_____

١٢ ازداد عدد الطلاب هذه السنة بصورة ملحوظة.

_____

١٣ أحب كل الألوان وأحب اللون الأزرق بصفة خاصة.

_____

١٤ ليس لدي صديق مفضل وأحب كل أصدقائي بشكل عام.

_____

١٥ يتكلم دائماً بهدوء.

_____

١٦ شعروا بالخوف عندما بدأ يتصرف بعنف.

_____

١٧ يحبون جدتهم لأنها تعاملهم بمحبة.

_____

١٨ تابعوا النقاش باهتمام كبير.

_____

١٩ تكلم بصورة عامة ولم يقدم أية أمثلة.

_____

٢٠ فهم معنى الكلمات اللاتينية بسهولة.

_____

Prepositional phrase as a fronted predicate

The sentence that includes a prepositional phrase as a fronted predicate is a nominal sentence as opposed to the verbal sentence. This sentence includes a **mubtada** and a **khabar**. In this kind of nominative sentences, the order is reversed, that is, the **khabar** is fronted because the subject is indefinite. The order of these two parts—**mubtada** and **khabar**—must be maintained because an Arabic sentence does not start with an indefinite noun.

This form of sentence has two major functions:

1. Descriptive: Prepositional phrases that function as fronted predicates are very common in certain statements, especially those related to defining place and time.

A park is behind the house. (Behind the house there is a park).	وراء البيت حديقة عامة.
A Syrian restaurant is near the library. (Near the library there is a Syrian restaurant).	قرب المكتبة مطعم سوري.
Our street is wide and there is a famous restaurant on it.	شارعنا واسع وفيه مطعم شهير.
There is a meeting for the students before the class. (Before the class there is a meeting for the students).	قبل الدرس اجتماع للطلاب.

2. Possessions, ownership, and affinities: These prepositional phrases mainly function in a similar way as the verb *to have* in English.

I have a friend in London.	لي صديق في لندن.
He has a new dictionary.	عنده قاموس جديد.
I have two tickets for the play.	معي بطاقتان للمسرحية.

EXERCISE

14·2

*John is a British student studying Arabic at the University of Damascus. He wrote the following e-mail to his Arab friend who lives in London. Identify the prepositional phrases that work like a fronted predicate, along with their subjects (subject of the nominal sentence, i.e., the **mubtada**), and then translate them into English.*

EXAMPLE

في البريد رسالة. fronted predicate: في البريد

subject of the nominal sentence (**mubtada**): رسالة

There is a letter in the mail.

١ في البداية، تحية لكَ ولأسرتكَ من دمشق.

_____

٢ أنا الآن أدرس العربية بجامعة دمشق، وهي جامعة كبيرة وفيها معهد للغة العربية.

_____

٣ جامعة دمشق جامعة شهيرة، ولها تاريخ.

_____

٤ ومعهد اللغة العربية له سمعة عالمية.

_____

٥ للمعهد مبنى كبير وحديث على أوتوستراد المزة.

_____

٦ وراء المبنى حديقة جميلة وفيها نافورة ماء.

_____

٧ حول النافورة طاولات ومقاعد.

_____

٨ وأمامه حديقة أخرى أصغر من السابقة.

_____

٩ في الطابق الأول من المبنى مكتب الاستقبال ومكاتب المدرسين.

_____

١٠ على يسار مكتب الاستقبال غرفة الحاسوب.

_____

١١ في الطابق الثاني غرف الصف.

_____

١٢ وفي الطابق الثالث الكافيتيريا والمكتبة.

_____

١٣ بين الكافيتيريا والمكتبة هاتف عمومي للطلاب.

_____

١٤ في الكافيتريا طاولات وكراسي.

_____

١٥ وعلى جدارها صور لدمشق القديمة.

_____

١٦ في المزة معاهد وفروع أخرى لجامعة دمشق.

_____

١٧ في المعهد أساتذة مشهورون من جميع الاختصاصات.

_____

١٨ أكتب لك هذه الرسالة الآن من غرفة الحاسوب.

_____

١٩ خارج المبنى ضجيج وأصوات سيارات.

_____

٢٠ ولكن داخل المبنى هدوء كامل.

_____

٢١ عند الظهر هناك استراحة لساعة أتناول فيها الغداء.

_____

٢٢ قبل الاستراحة درس في الإعلام العربي.

_____

٢٣ وبعد الاستراحة درس في الشعر الكلاسيكي.

_____

٢٤ فوق طاولتي رواية لحنا مينة.

_____

٢٥ بين صف القواعد وصف الأدب في المساء استراحة طويلة أقرأ فيها عادة.

_____

٢٦ وتحت طاولتي حقيبة جميلة اشتريتها من سوق الصناعات اليدوية أمس.

_____

٢٧ في دمشق الكثير من الأسواق التقليدية و المتاحف الشهيرة.

_____

٢٨ سأعود بعد قليل إلى غرفتي.

_____

٢٩ في المساء حفلة جميلة سأحضرها مع أصدقائي.

_____

٣٠ للجميع سلامي.

_____

EXERCISE 14·3

Identify the prepositional phrases that function like a fronted predicate along with their subjects. Translate the sentences into English.

EXAMPLE
عندهم بيت كبير في شمال المدينة.

They have a big house in the north of the city.

١ له أصدقاء كثيرون في مصر.

_____

٢ عندنا امتحان في اللغة العربية الأسبوع القادم.

_____

٣ معي كتب كثيرة.

_____

٤ لصديقتي عم في أمريكا.

_____

٥ صديقتي لها عم غني جداً في أمريكا.

_____

٦ عندهم بيت جميل.

_____

٧ معنا بعض الأصدقاء.

_____

٨ لصديقي ثلاثة أخوة.

_____

٩ صديقي له ثلاثة أخوة.

_____

١٠ زميلك مصاب بالرشح، هل معك منديل؟

_____

١١ هل عندك سيارة؟

_____

Adverbial and prepositional phrases in the negative

The phrases that start with عند, مع can be negated by the negative article ما. But all prepositional phrases can be negated with the more formal semiverb ليس that directly precedes the prepositional phrase.

	ما عندي أية مواعيد هذا الأسبوع.
I do not have any appointments this week.	ليس عندي أية مواعيد هذا الأسبوع.
	ما معه عادة إلا حقيبة واحدة.
Usually, he only has one bag with him.	ليس معه عادة إلا حقيبة واحدة.

ليس directly precedes the prepositional phrase.

	لجارتي صديقة: ليس لجارتي صديقة.
My neighbor has a friend: my neighbor does not have a friend.	جارتي لها صديقة: جارتي ليس لها صديقة.

Negate the following sentences.

EXAMPLE   في الكتاب صورة. (There is a picture in the book.)

ليس في الكتاب صورة. (There isn't a picture in the book.)

١ بعد الاستراحة درس في اللغة العربية.

_____

٢ فوق طاولتي رواية.

_____

٣ بين صف القواعد وصف الأدب في المساء استراحة.

_____

٤ تحت طاولتي حقيبة.

_____

٥ في المساء حفلة.

_____

٦ له أصدقاء كثيرون.

_____

٧ عندنا امتحان الأسبوع القادم.

_____

٨ معي كتب كثيرة.

_____

٩ لصديقتي أقارب يعملون في الخليج.

_____

١٠ صديقتي لها أقارب يعملون في الخليج.

_____

١١ لصديقي مساعد وسكرتيرة.

_____

١٢ صديقي له مساعد وسكرتيرة.

_____

Prepositional phrases in the past tense

These prepositional phrases can be put in the past tense by using كان. The verb can be conjugated and have the feminine form كانت. However, the verb in this context is impersonal and can be used for both genders in certain contexts.

He has a car.	عنده سيارة.
He used to have a car.	كان عنده سيارة.

The prepositional phrases in the past tense are semiverbal sentences. Therefore, they can be negated in the same manner as other usual verbal phrases in Arabic.

He didn't have a car.	ما كان عنده سيارة.
He did not have a car.	لم يكن عنده سيارة.

EXERCISE
14·5

Put the twelve sentences of Exercise 14.4 in the past tense and then negate them.

EXAMPLE   (There was a picture in the book.) كان في الكتاب صورة.

(There was no picture in the book.) لم يكن في الكتاب صورة.

_____ ١

_____ ٢

_____ ٣

_____ ٤

_____ ٥

_____ ٦

_____ ٧

_____ ٨

_____ ٩

_____

_____ ١٠

_____

_____ ١١

_____

_____ ١٢

_____

Prepositional phrases in the future tense

These prepositional phrases can refer to the future by using سوف, ـس. The verb is impersonal and can be used for both genders.

| I will have a car next year. | سيكون عندي سيارة السنة القادمة. |
| I will not have a car next year. | لن يكون عندي سيارة السنة القادمة. |

EXERCISE
14·6

Put the twelve sentences of Exercise 14.4 in the future tense and then negate them

EXAMPLE ستكون في الكتاب صورة. (There will be a picture in the book.)

لن تكون في الكتاب صورة. (There won't be a picture in the book.)

_____ ١

_____

_____ ٢

_____

_____ ٣

_____

_____ ٤

_____

_____ ٥

_____

_____ ٦

_____

_____ ٧

_____

_____ ٨

_____

_____ ٩

_____

_____ ١٠

_____

_____ ١١

_____

_____ ١٢

_____

The prepositional phrase as a hal

The prepositional sentence of **hal** takes the same form of a fronted predicate that was explained earlier in this chapter. However, it is here preceded by the و of the **hal**, which in Arabic is called **waw al-hal**. The sentence that follows **waw al-hal** is called the sentence of **hal** and it is a complete independent unit.

He waited for her with a rose in his hand.

انتظرها وفي يده وردة.

She stood at the door with a smile on her face.

وقفت على الباب وعلى وجهها ابتسامة.

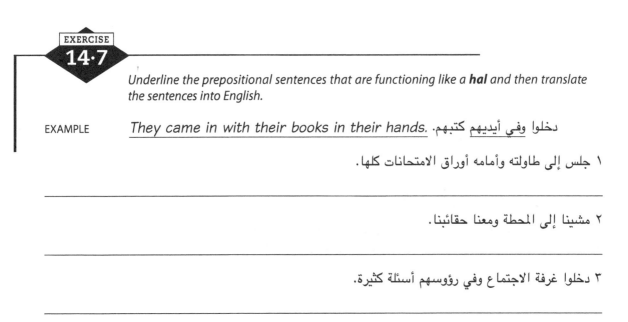

EXERCISE

14·7

Underline the prepositional sentences that are functioning like a **hal** and then translate the sentences into English.

EXAMPLE

They came in with their books in their hands. دخلوا وفي أيديهم كتبهم.

١ جلس إلى طاولته وأمامه أوراق الامتحانات كلها.

_____

٢ مشينا إلى المحطة ومعنا حقائبنا.

_____

٣ دخلوا غرفة الاجتماع وفي رؤوسهم أسئلة كثيرة.

_____

٤ جئت وفي نيتي أن أعتذر لكم.

_____

٥ غادر بلاده وبجيبه ألف ليرة فقط.

_____

٦ رحل وفي قلبه سر كبير.

_____

٧ نام وتحت مخدته صورتها.

_____

٨ خرجوا من المطعم وعلى طاولتهم الكثير من الطعام.

_____

٩ جلس في المكتبة ومن حوله طلابه.

_____

١٠ بدأت العمل ولي من العمر عشرون سنة.

_____

١١ قطعوا الصحراء ووصلوا وعلى ثيابهم وجوههم غبار.

_____

١٢ يخططون لمستقبل ناجح ويتقدمون وفي عقولهم مشاريع كبيرة.

_____

١٣ ذهبت إلى العمل وفي حقيبتي كل الأوراق.

_____

١٤ دخلنا البيت وعلى ثيابنا ومظلاتنا مياه المطر.

_____

١٥ نام في الطريق وإلى جانبه كلبه.

_____

Prepositions with verbs

When prepositions are combined with verbs they can influence the function, form, and meaning of the verbs. The following two categories have the most common patterns.

Using prepositions to change intransitive verbs

Intransitive verbs in Arabic, especially verbs of motions, can be made transitive through a preposition.

to go with the book, to take the book away	ذهب بالكتاب

And transitive verbs with direct object can have a second indirect object through a preposition.

to come with, to bring along	جاء بـ
He brought his friend a beautiful present on his birthday.	جاء صديقه بهدية جميلة في عيد ميلاده.

Here are some of the verbs that can be made transitive or have two objects if they are followed by a preposition.

he brought	أتى بـ
he brought	حضر بـ
he brought	قدم بـ

EXERCISE
14·8

Translate the following sentences into English.

EXAMPLE   *He brought me his book.* جاءني بكتابه.

١ جاء بأوراق الاجتماع.

_____

٢ دخل الغرفة بحقائبه الكثيرة.

_____

٣ أتانا بالأخبار السعيدة عن الوطن.

_____

٤ سافر إلى بلده بحقيبة واحدة.

_____

٥ صعد الطائرة بحقيبتين في يديه.

_____

٦ مضى إليهم بالأخبار.

_____

٧ قدم بقصص جديدة.

_____

٨ وصل إلى حفلة عيد ميلاد زميله بصديقته.

_____

Suppressed verbs

In certain exclamations the preposition indicates the existence of a suppressed verb.

welcome to you	مرحباً بك
I welcome you	أرحب بك

EXERCISE
14·9

Underline the prepositional phrase that indicates the presence of a suppressed verb and translate the sentences into English.

EXAMPLE

ختم الرسالة بالقول: "مع حبي."

He concluded his letter by saying, "with my love."

١ قلنا لهم إننا سنزورهم غداً بعد أن ننتهي من العمل فقالوا: "أهلا بكن."

_____

٢ قالت الأستاذة للطلاب عندما نجحوا في اختبار اللغة العربية: "مرحى لكم."

_____

٣ نحن سعداء بمجيئكم. مرحبا بكم وبأصدقائكم الأعزاء الذين جاؤوا معكم.

_____

٤ عندما مر في الطريق رآهم جالسين أمام باب البيت فقال لهم: "السلام عليكم."

_____

٥ أنت مهندس عظيم! تحية لكَ ولكل من عملوا معكَ في هذا المشروع الناجح.

_____

٦ سأتصل بك غداً وأنت في طريقك إلى المطار لأقول لك مع السلامة.

_____

٧ عندما خرجت من البيت مشى والدي ورائي وهو يقول: "بأمان الله."

_____

Prepositional phrases as **nisba** adjectives

This is one of the subcategories of Arabic adjectives. **Nisba** adjectives have several functions according to their references. The examples below represent some of the major areas in which the **nisba** adjective is used. They can refer to nationalities and to other places of origin such as regions and towns.

Iraqi: from Iraq	عراقي: من العراق
Qudsi: from al-Quds	قدسي: من القدس
Shami: from Al-Sham (Greater Syria)	شامي: من الشام

They can also refer to ethnicities and affinities to ethnic or religious communities.

Orthodox: from the Orthodox denomination	أرثوذكسي: من طائفة الأرثوذكس
Shia: from the Shia denomination	شيعي: من مذهب الشيعة

They can also refer to affinities with institutions.

Academic: from university	جامعي: من الجامعة
Parliamentary: related to/from the Parliament	برلماني: من البرلمان

As the preceding examples indicate, this information can also be expressed by prepositional phrases using the preposition من. The main process is to drop the suffixes. Sometimes, no other change is needed (first category).

We are Aleppine: we are from Aleppo.	نحن حلبيون: نحن من حلب.
They are Lebanese: they are from Lebanon.	هما لبنانيان: هم من لبنان.

The second category requires some minor adjustments such as reinstating the definite article "al."

You are Moroccan (d. m.): you are from Morocco.	أنتما مغربيان: أنتما من المغرب.
He is Iraqi: he is from Iraq.	هو عراقي: هو من العراق.

The third category requires restoring the **ta' marbuta** at the end of the word.

You are Gazan (s. m.): you are from Gaza.	أنتَ غزي: أنتَ من غزة.
You are Cairean (s. f.): you are from Cairo.	أنتِ قاهرية: أنتِ من القاهرة.

The fourth one requires restoring the **ya'** and **alif**.

I am Syrian: I am from Syria.	أنا سوري: أنا من سوريا.
You are Libyan (s. m.): you are from Libya.	أنتَ ليبي: أنتَ من ليبيا.

The fifth category requires restoring the **ya'** and **ta' marbuta**.

They are Saudis (pl. m.): they are from Saudi Arabia.	هم سعوديون: هم من السعودية.
They are Alexandrian (pl. f.): they are from Alexandria.	هن اسكندريات: هن من الاسكندرية.

Use the pronouns and the names of countries and the information about gender in order to define the origins of these people by using **nisba** adjectives and then by using prepositional sentences.

EXAMPLE   هو، دمشق. <u>هو دمشقي. هو من دمشق.</u>

He is Damascene. He is from Damascus.

١ هنّ، موريتانيا

_____

٢ هما، مراكش (.m)

_____

٣ نحن، البحرين (.f)

_____

٣ هو، مصر

_____

٥ أنا، الشام (.f)

_____

٦ أنا، الإمارات (.m)

_____

٧ هما، الأردن (.f)

_____

٨ هم، الصعيد

_____

٩ أنتم، الكويت

_____

١٠ هنّ، اليمن

_____

١١ نحن، السودان (.f)

_____

١٢ هو، قطر

_____

١٣ هما، الجزائر (.m)

_____

١٤ أنا، تونس (.m)

_____

EXERCISE 14·11

Fill in the blanks in the following sentences and translate them into English.

EXAMPLE

فرانسيس مراش الحلبي روائي سوري من القرن التاسع عشر وسارة الحلبية شاعرة أندلسية
من القرن الثالث عشر، وكلاهما بالأصل من مدينة <u>حلب</u> السورية.

Francis Al-Marrash Al-Halabi is a nineteenth century Syrian novelist
and Sarah Al-Halabiyya is an Andalusian poetess from the thirteenth
century, and both of them are originally from the Syrian city of Aleppo.

١ المقام البغدادي هو من الفنون الموسيقية العربية القديمة التي تطورت على يد فنانين من _____.

_____

٢ أبو العبد البيروتي شخصية شعبية خيالية لبنانية لحكواتي ظريف يعيش في _____.

_____

٣ المغنية المشهورة علية التونسية هي من رائدات الغناء الشعبي العربي و هي بالأصل من _____.

_____

٤ عائلة المفكر الشهير ألبرت حوراني منتشرة في بلاد الشام كلها، ولكن العائلة بالأصل من سهل
_____ في جنوب سوريا.

_____

٥ عمل القديس يوحنا التغلبي الدمشقي وزيرا للأمويين. هو بالأصل من قبيلة تغلب التي انتشرت حول الفرات في
سوريا، لكن عائلته من _____.

_____

٦ الكاتب التليفزيوني الشهير لينين الرملي مصري، ولكن أجداده من مدينة _____ في فلسطين.

_____

٧ المطربة المشهورة وردة الجزائرية سكنت واشتهرت في مصر، ولكنها بالأصل من _____.

_____

Different functions of prepositional phrases **127**

٨ الملكة نور الحسين زوجة ملك الأردن الراحل الملك حسين. كان اسمها قبل الزواج نور الحلبي. أمها أمريكية ووالدها من مدينة ــــــــــــــ في سوريا.

_____

_____

٩ ديك الجن الحمصي شاعر عربي معروف اشتهر بقصائده حول حبيبته ورد. عاش ديك الجن طوال حياته في مدينة ــــــــــــــ.

_____

_____

١٠ عاش العالم الشهير الحسن البصري في القرن السابع في مدينة ــــــــــــــ بالعراق.

_____

_____

١١ عائلة حجازي منتشرة في مدينتي الرياض وجدة، ولكنها أتت بالأصل من منطقة ــــــــــــــ بالسعودية.

_____

_____

١٢ داود الأنطاكي عالم سوري شهير له كتب في الطب والفلك، وهو من ــــــــــــــ.

_____

_____

١٣ من الأقمشة العربية الشهيرة التي استخدمها الأوربيون عبر القرون الوسطى الموسلين، أي القماش الموصلي بالعربية، وهو قماش كان يصنع في مدينة ــــــــــــــ بالعراق.

_____

_____

١٤ أما قماش الدامسكو الشهير الذي كان استخدم تاريخيا لصنع ثياب النبلاء ورجال الدين فاسمه بالعربية يعني القماش الدمشقي، وقد كان يصنع في مدينة ــــــــــــــ بسوريا.

_____

_____

Prepositional phrases as a replacement for other parts of speech

Prepositional phrases can be used as a replacement for other parts of speech in many instances. The following are the four major ones.

Specification for tamyiz

Prepositional phrases can be used as a replacement of a specification for **tamyiz**.

He worked the whole night so he collapsed out
of exhaustion.

عمل طوال الليل فانهار تعباً.

He collapsed out of exhaustion.

انهار من التعب.

EXERCISE 14·12

*Identify the **tamyiz** in the following sentences. Turn them into prepositional phrases and translate them into English.*

EXAMPLE

شعر كأنه سينهار عطشاً. شعر كأنه سينهار مبم العطش.

He felt as if he will collapse out of thirst.

١ الغرفة باردة جدا نكاد نتجمد برداً.

_____

_____

٢ لم يأكل شيئا منذ الصباح وهو يحس أنه يكاد يموت جوعاً.

_____

_____

٣ عندما سمع النتيجة احمر غضباً.

_____

_____

٤ عندما رأت الكلب اصفرت خوفاً.

_____

_____

٥ عندما سمع الخبر طار فرحاً.

_____

_____

٦ عندما خسر اللعبة بكى ندماً.

_____

_____

٧ عندما شاهدت الفيلم سالت دموعها حزناً.

_____

_____

٨ عندما شرب الزجاجة وقع أرضاً.

_____

_____

٩ عندما ضربه الولد صاح ألماً.

_____

_____

١٠ ابيض شعره شيئاً عندما كبر في السن.

_____

_____

Specification for mafu'l li ajlihi

Prepositional phrases can be used as a replacement of specification for **mafu'l li ajlihi**, which provides the reason as to why the action took place.

He came to the city out of desire to be far   جاء المدينة رغبة بالابتعاد عن قريته.
from his village.

EXERCISE
14·13

*Identify the **mafu'l li ajlihi** in the following sentences. Translate them into English and then turn them into prepositional phrases.*

EXAMPLE   غيرت ثيابها <u>استعدادا للخروج</u>.

She changed her clothes in preparation to go out.

غيرت ثيابها للاستعداد للخروج

١ درست اللغة الفرنسية حبا بالشعر الفرنسي.

_____

_____

٢ جاء إلى لندن طلبا للدراسة.

_____

_____

٣ سافر إلى دبي رغبة بالحصول على عمل.

_____

_____

٤ لبست معطفها خوفاً من البرد.

_____

_____

٥ انتظر أمام بيتها أملاً أن يراها.

_____

_____

٦ غطت شعرها اتقاء للمطر.

_____

_____

٧ درس الطلاب استعداداً للامتحان.

_____

_____

٨ لن نمر من مركز المدينة تحاشياً للازدحام.

_____

_____

٩ درس الأدب الانكليزي عشقاً لشكسبير.

_____

_____

١٠ يعمل في التلفزيون سعياً وراء الشهرة.

_____

_____

١١ يحاولون التقرب منه طمعاً بأمواله.

_____

_____

١٢ أفرغ كل خزاناته بحثاً عن الصورة الضائعة.

_____

_____

Replacement of adjectives

Prepositional phrases can be used as a replacement for adjectives.

a wooden table	طاولة خشبية
a wooden table (or made of wood)	طاولة من الخشب

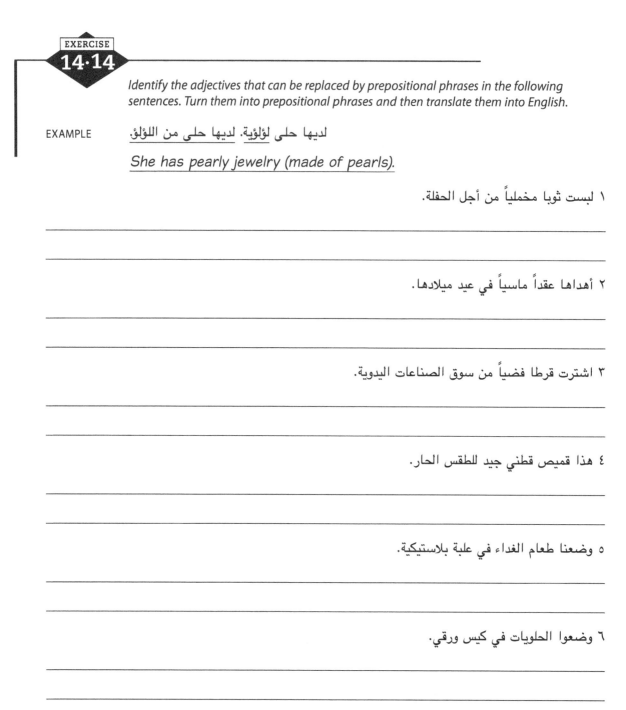

EXERCISE
14·14

Identify the adjectives that can be replaced by prepositional phrases in the following sentences. Turn them into prepositional phrases and then translate them into English.

EXAMPLE   لديها حلى لؤلؤية. لديها حلى من اللؤلؤ.

She has pearly jewelry (made of pearls).

١ لبست ثوبا مخملياً من أجل الحفلة.

_____

_____

٢ أهداها عقداً ماسياً في عيد ميلادها.

_____

_____

٣ اشترت قرطا فضياً من سوق الصناعات اليدوية.

_____

_____

٤ هذا قميص قطني جيد للطقس الحار.

_____

_____

٥ وضعنا طعام الغداء في علبة بلاستيكية.

_____

_____

٦ وضعوا الحلويات في كيس ورقي.

_____

_____

٧ سألبس كنزة صوفية لأن الطقس بارد.

_____

_____

٨ تلبس عباءة حريرية سوداء عندما تذهب إلى السعودية.

_____

_____

٩ وضعت في يدها سواراً ذهبياً.

_____

_____

١٠ سيحيطون حديقتهم بسور حديدي.

_____

_____

١١ أعطتها جدتها ملعقة نحاسية.

_____

_____

١٢ هو شخص قاس وله قلب حجري.

_____

_____

Other uses of من

من is a preposition that can introduce a sentence when followed by a descriptive term such as a participle or an adjective. It is a common construction in Arabic that expresses an introductory observation and indicates objectivity without defining the source of information or as a general knowledge.

It is difficult to get a job in this country.	من الصعب الحصول على وظيفة في هذه البلد.
It is possible to get a job in this country.	من الممكن الحصول على وظيفة في هذه البلد.
It is necessary to study for the exam.	من الضروري أن ندرس للامتحان.

Identify the words that you can turn into participles and adjectives. Turn the specific and personal statements into more objective statements by using the preposition من. Translate the sentences into English.

EXAMPLE

<u>أعتقد</u> أنه سيحصل على الجائزة.

<u>من المعتقد</u> أنه سيحصل على الجائزة. *It is believed that he will receive the award.*

١ ستحصل بسهولة على قبول في الجامعة بعد الحصول على المنحة.

_____

_____

٢ الوصول إلى المسرح بدون سيارة صعب.

_____

_____

٣ نتوقع وصول الوزير غداً.

_____

_____

٤ قرر الرئيس أن يقوم بزيارة رسمية إلى أمريكا.

_____

_____

٥ يلزمنا أن نعود إلى البيت عند الغداء.

_____

_____

٦ إن عقد اجتماع هذا الشهر أمر محتمل.

_____

_____

٧ حضور حفلة مع الأصدقاء القدامى أمر رائع.

_____

_____

٨ يمكننا أن نذهب إلى السينما يوم الجمعة.

_____

_____

٩ غسل اليدين قبل تناول الطعام ضروري.

_____

_____

١٠ يهمهم احترام زملاء العمل.

_____

_____

Prepositions with interrogative and relative pronouns

Prepositions with interrogative pronouns

When certain prepositions are followed by the interrogative pronouns (question particles) من؟ or وماذا؟ they are joined together in one compound particle. These compound particles take the following abbreviated forms.

	١ إلى ماذا = إلامَ؟
What are you aiming at (what do you mean)?	إلامَ ترمي في حديثك؟
	٢ بـ ماذا = بمَ؟
With what do you wash your hair? With shampoo or with soap?	بمَ تغسلين شعرك؟ بالشامبو أم بالصابون؟
	٣ بـ من = بمن؟
Whom do you trust?	بمن تثق؟
	٤ على ماذا = علامَ؟
What are you fighting about/over?	علامَ تتقاتلون؟
	٥ عن ماذا؟ = عمَ؟
I did not understand a word of his talk. What is he talking about?	لم أفهم كلمة من حديثه. عمَ يتكلم؟
	٦ عن من = عمن؟
Who is the man who knocked at the door asking about?	عمن يسأل الرجل الذي قرع الباب؟
	٧ في ماذا = فيمَ؟
What are you thinking about?	فيمَ تفكر؟
	٨ في من = فيمن؟
Who are you thinking about?	فيمن تفكر؟
	٩ لـ ماذا = لِمَ؟
Why did you change your mind?	لِمَ غيرت رأيك؟
	١٠ لـ من = لمن؟
Whom did you give the book to?	لمن أعطيت الكتاب؟

135

١١ من ماذا؟ = مم؟

What are you complaining about?

مم تشكو؟

١٢ من من = ممن؟

Who did you take this money from?

ممن أخذت هذه النقود؟

EXERCISE
15·1

Formulate a question for each of the following answers using a compound particle that combines the preposition إلى and an interrogative pronoun. Translate the new sentences into English.

EXAMPLE

نظرت من النافذة إلى الناس في الشارع.

(I looked at the people in the street from the window.)

إلام نظرت من الشباك؟ *What did you look at from the window?*

١ ترمز الوردة الحمراء إلى الحب القوي.

_____

_____

٢ يعود الغريب إلى بلاده.

_____

_____

٣ سيؤدي هذا النقاش إلى اتفاق.

_____

_____

٤ أنظر إلى اللوحة.

_____

_____

٥ هذا الشارع يأخذنا إلى الحديقة العامة.

_____

_____

٦ المحاضر يلمح إلى إمكانية إنهاء الصراع.

_____

_____

٧ إشارة المرور هذه تشير إلى شارع عريض.

_____

_____

٨ يلتفت الطفل إلى أمه عندما تتكلم.

_____

_____

*Translate the following sentences into English and then formulate a question for each
of the following answers using a compound particle that combines the preposition ﺑ
and an interrogative pronoun.*

EXAMPLE   قطعت الكعكة بالسكين. *I cut the cake with a knife.*

بم قطعت الكعكة؟

١ كتبت الوظيفة هذا المساء بالقلم الجديد.

_____

_____

٢ يتسلى الموظفون بألعاب الكومبيوتر عندما يكون لديهم استراحة في المكتب

_____

_____

٣ أتصل بأهلي وأصدقائي عندما أشعر بالوحدة.

_____

_____

٤ رسم الفنان اللوحة الشهيرة باللونين الأبيض والأسود.

_____

_____

٥ أستعين بإخوتي حين أواجه في مشكلة.

_____

_____

٦ اجتمع المدير الجديد بالموظفين اليوم.

_____

_____

Prepositions with interrogative and relative pronouns   **137**

٧ يلعب أطفالي مع أصدقائهم بعد المدرسة بالكرة التي اشتروها الشهر الماضي.

_____

_____

٨ يحتفل الناس في الواحد والثلاثين من شهر كانون الثاني (ديسمبر) بقدوم السنة الجديدة.

_____

_____

٩ التقيت بأصدقاء طفولتي عندما سافرت إلى قريتي الشهر الماضي.

_____

_____

١٠ أنظف يدي بالماء والصابون(s. m.) .

_____

_____

Formulate a question for each of the following answers using a compound particle that combines the preposition على and an interrogative pronoun.

EXAMPLE

وقف الطفل على الكرسي. (The child stood on the chair.)

علام وقف الطفل؟ (What did the child stand on?)

١ اتفق الفريقان على احترام حقوق بعضهم البعض.

_____

٢ هذا الطفل يبكي على أمه التي ذهبت إلى المطبخ.

_____

٣ يتنافسون على جائزة قيمة.

_____

٤ يدل هذا التصرف على رغبة بحل المشاكل.

_____

٥ تجيب هذه الجملة على سؤال عن قواعد الضمائر وحروف الجر.

_____

٦ يفاوضون على حق شعبهم في دولة مستقلة.

_____

٧ أعتمد في تقييمي للطلاب على أدائهم في الصف والامتحان. (s. m.)

_____

Translate the following sentences into English and then formulate a question for each answer using a compound particle that combines the preposition عن and an interrogative pronoun.

EXAMPLE   تحدث الأستاذ عن كتابه المفضل. *The teacher talked about his favorite book.*

عم تحدث الأستاذ؟ (What did the teacher talk about?)

١ أبعدت الأم القطة عن الطفل.

_____

_____

٢ يجب إبعاد الطفل عن الموقد.

_____

_____

٣ سأسأل عن كل أصدقاء طفولتي عندما أزور مسقط رأسي.

_____

_____

٤ سيكتب الصحفي المقالة عن نجيب محفوظ.

_____

_____

٥ سألت الرجل في الطريق عن محطة القطار.

_____

_____

٦ تكلم المحاضر عن العلاقات العربية-الأوربية.

_____

_____

٧ أفرجت الشرطة اليوم عن بعض المعتقلين السياسيين.

_____

_____

٨ يبحثون عن حلول لمشاكلهم.

_____

_____

٩ سيتحدث الأستاذ عن سعد الله ونوس في محاضرته عن المسرح العربي.

_____

_____

١٠ أشبه أبي وأمي، لكني أختلف عن أبي من ناحية الشكل.

_____

_____

١١ يدافع عن حقه في العودة إلى بلاده.

_____

_____

١٢ تعبر هذه القصيدة عن حب الشاعر للطبيعة.

_____

_____

Formulate a question for each of the following answers using a compound particle that combines the preposition في and an interrogative pronoun.

EXAMPLE

يفكرون في الامتحان. (They are thinking about the exam.)

<u>فيم يفكرون؟</u> (What are they thinking about?)

١ يفكر طوال الوقت في مستقبله.

_____

٢ سأضع كل هذه الكتب في حقيبتي الكبيرة.

_____

٣ تورطوا في مشكلة صعبة.

_____

٤ أضع ثقتي في أهلي وأصدقائي.

_____

٥ سنشارك خلال المهرجان في عزف الموسيقى.

_____

٦ تفكر في حبيبها.

_____

٧ سأجري بحثي القادم في الفنون الشعبية.

_____

Formulate a question for each of the following answers using a compound particle that combines the preposition ـل and an interrogative pronoun.

EXAMPLE   (He sent the flowers to his wife.) أرسل الورود لزوجته.

(Who did he send the flowers to?) <u>لمن أرسل الورود؟</u>

١ هذه السيارة للمدير.

_____

٢ انتقلت من بيتي القديم الجميل لأكون قريباً من مكان عملي.

_____

٣ سأعطي كتبي القديمة للمكتبة العامة.

_____

٤ سأرسل كل هذه البطاقات البريدية لأصدقائي في عيد الميلاد.

_____

٥ أمشي بسرعة لأنني تأخرت على عملي.

_____

٦ لم أتصل بكم لأنني كنت في عمل خارج المدينة.

_____

٧ ألوح بيدي لجارتي الجالسة في شرفة بيتها.

_____

٨ أنا حزين لأن أصدقائي سيسافرون إلى بلدانهم في العطلة.

_____

٩ ألبس كل هذه الثياب لأن الطقس سيصبح بارداً جدا في المساء.

_____

١٠ يبيع هذا الولد المجوهرات التقليدية للسياح.

_____

Formulate a question for each of the following answers using a compound particle that combines the preposition من and an interrogative pronoun.

EXAMPLE   تلقت هذه الورود من زوجها. (She received these flowers from her husband.)

ممن تلقت هذه الورود؟ (Who did she receive these flowers from?)

١ استعرت هذا القلم من زميلي في الصف.

_____

٢ آخذ مصروفي الشهري عادة من والدي.

_____

٣ صنع هذا العقد الجميل من المجوهرات التقليدية.

_____

٤ يغير بيته كثيراً لأنه يريد الهروب من الشرطة.

_____

٥ إذا وقعت في مشكلة، سأطلب المساعدة من أصدقائي وأهلي.

_____

٦ صنعت هذه الكعكة اللذيذة من الحليب والبيض.

_____

٧ أخاف عندما أمشي في الغابة من حيوانات الغابة.

_____

٨ تلقيت هذه الرسالة من صديقة طفولتي.

_____

Prepositions with relative pronouns

When certain prepositions are followed by the relative pronouns ما or من they are joined together in one compound particle. These compound particles take the following abbreviated forms.

١   بـ ما = بما

Do not tell anybody about   لا تخبر أحدا بما قلته لكَ.
what I have told you.

٢   بـ من = بمن

Call those who asked about you   اتصل بمن سألوا عنك عندما كنت في العمل.
when you were at work.

٣ عن ما = عما

Tell me about what you have seen
on your trip.

حدثني عما رأيت في رحلتك.

٤ عن من = عمن

Tell me about who you met at
the party.

حدثني عمن التقيت في الحفلة.

٥ في ما = فيما

He's the one responsible for your
current situation.

هو جعلكم تقعون فيما أنتم فيه الآن.

٦ في من = فيمن

I put my trust in those who put their
trust in me.

أضع ثقتي فيمن يضع ثقته بي.

٧ لـ ما = لما

I was saddened because of what
happened to you.

حزنت لما حدث لكم.

٨ لـ من = لمن

I provide my help to whoever needs it.

أقدم مساعدتي لمن يحتاجها.

٩ من ما = مما

I am also afraid of what you are afraid of.

أنا أيضا خائف مما أنت خائف منه.

EXERCISE
15·8

*Underline the compound particles that combine the relative pronoun من or ما with
a preposition in the following sentences. Translate the sentences into English and formulate
a question in Arabic for each of these statements.*

EXAMPLE

I heard the good news from my manager. سمعت الأخبار السارة من المدير.

(Who did you hear the good news from?) ممن سمعت الأخبار السارة؟

١ صنعت كعكة عيد ميلادها مما اشترته من السوق.

_____

_____

٢ استعدت الكتاب ممن استعاره مني.

_____

_____

٣ سأنصح أطفالي بما نصحني به أبي.

_____

_____

٤ أخبرهم عما ينوي فعله.

_____

_____

٥ أنا مستغرب مما قالوه.

_____

_____

٦ معي من النقود أكثر مما معك.

_____

_____

٧ عندما يقع خلاف بين أصدقائي، أدافع دوما عمن يحتاجني أكثر.

_____

_____

٨ أفكر فيما قلته الآن.

_____

_____

٩ حدثناهم عما فعلنا البارحة.

_____

_____

١٠ يضع أمله فيمن يحبه من أهله أصدقائه.

_____

_____

١١ نعم، تعلم اللغة اللاتينية أصعب مما كنت أظن.

_____

_____

١٢ شاهدوا فيلم رعب في التلفزيون وهم خائفون مما شاهدوه.

_____

_____

١٣ أثق بمن يثق بي.

_____

_____

١٤ غضب جارنا مما قلناه له.

_____

_____

١٥ أعط الكتب لمن يحتاجها.

_____

_____

١٦ عند عودتي سأسأل عمن سأل عني.

_____

_____

١٧ صديقي المريض يشكو مما يشكو منه والده.

_____

_____

١٨ لم يستجب المدير لما طلبه الموظفون.

_____

_____

١٩ لا، فدراسة اللغات أصعب مما توقعت.

_____

_____

٢٠ استمتعنا بما قدموه من رقصات وما عزفوه من موسيقى.

_____

_____

Practicing prepositions in context

Congratulations! You have completed reading the book and achieved a lot. Here are two texts for your final practice with prepositions.

Text I: My room

A new student in the Arabic department is describing his room as follows:

اسمي جون وأنا من مدينة نيويورك. أدرس اللغة العربية في معهد اللغات في جامعة دمشق. أسكن مع جورج وهو طالب من بريطانيا. انتقلت منذ أسبوع إلى غرفتي الجديدة. تقع الغرفة في بيت كبير وسط المدينة القديمة خلف الجامع الأموي. في وسط البيت حديقة صغيرة فيها بركة ونافورة ماء نشرب قربها القهوة في الصباح ونسهر حولها في الليل. على يمين البركة شجرة ياسمين وعلى يسارها شجرة ليمون. أمام البيت مقهى شعبي ألتقي فيه مع أصدقائي، وقربه مطعم صغير وهناك عدة محلات لبيع التحف حوله.

EXERCISE

16·1

Translate Text I into English.

EXAMPLE   غرفتي. _My room._

١ اسمي جون.

_____

٢ وأنا من مدينة نيويورك.

_____

٣ أدرس اللغة العربية في معهد اللغات في جامعة دمشق.

_____

٤ أسكن مع جورج وهو طالب من بريطانيا.

_____

٥ انتقلت منذ أسبوع إلى غرفتي الجديدة.

_____

٦ تقع الغرفة في بيت كبير وسط المدينة القديمة خلف الجامع الأموي.

_____

٧ في وسط البيت حديقة صغيرة فيها بركة ونافورة ماء نتناول قربها القهوة في الصباح ونسهر حولها في الليل.

_____

٨ على يمين البركة شجرة ياسمين وعلى يسارها شجرة ليمون.

_____

٩ أمام البيت مقهى شعبي ألتقي فيه مع أصدقائي.

_____

١٠ وقربه مطعم صغير وهناك عدة محلات لبيع التحف حوله.

_____

List the prepositional phrases in Text I.

_____

_____

_____

_____

Categorize the prepositions in Text I into single and compound particles (identify the compound ones as combined with an attached pronoun) and adverbs of time and place.

EXAMPLE   اشتريت الجريدة من محل بجانب الجامعة واشتريت منه مجلة أيضاً.

single particle-preposition: من

preposition compound with a dharf (adverb of place): بجانب

preposition compound with an attached pronoun: منه

_____ ١

_____ ٢

_____ ٣

_____ ٤

_____ ٥

_____ ٦

_____ ٧

_____ ٨

_____ ٩

_____ ١٠

_____ ١١

_____ ١٢

_____ ١٣

_____ ١٤

_____ ١٥

_____ ١٦

_____ ١٧

Text II: A vacation in Tartous

اتصل بي اليوم صديقي أيمن الذي يدرس معي في المدرسة الابتدائية وقال: "تبدو سعيداً جداً، لماذا؟"

قلت له: "لأننا مسافرون."

قال: "إلى أين؟"

قلت له: "أنا الآن مشغول. سأكتب لكَ رسالة إلكترونية بعد قليل."

قال: "ومتى ستعودون؟"

قلت: "لا أعرف." بعد دقائق كتبت له هذه الرسالة وأرسلتها بالبريد الإلكتروني:

"أنا سعيد جدا هذا الصباح. بدأت اليوم عطلة أبي الصيفية. ستسافر عائلتي إلى مدينة طرطوس غداً لقضاء أسبوعين في المدينة وعلى شاطئها كما نفعل كل سنة. خرج أبي باكراً ليحجز تذاكر سفرنا. وضعت أمي في حقيبتنا الكبيرة ملابسي وملابس أخوتي الصيفية وثياب سباحتنا وألعابنا المائية و آلات تصويرنا بالإضافة إلى كل ما اشتراه أبي للعطلة.

طرطوس مدينة فينيقية جميلة واسمها الفينيقي "أرادوس." البحر في تلك المدينة جميل وأمواجه زرقاء. أنا وأخوتي ووالدي نقضي يومنا عادة في السباحة في البحر وبناء بيوت على رمله، بينما تشرب أمي قهوتها، وهي تنظر إلينا من تحت المظلة. كلنا نحب السمك ولذلك نقضي وقت الغداء في المطاعم الجبلية أو في جزيرة أرواد حيث نتناوله ونحن نستمتع بالطبيعة هناك.

في المساء ننزل إلى المدينة ونتمشى في شوارعها أو نزور أقارينا وكل من يدعونا من أصدقاء والدي. ونخرج معهم أحيانا إلى المطاعم والمقاهي."

You have read this text at the end of Part I and identified its pronouns. It comprises references to most grammatical rules concerning the different kinds of prepositions that you have learned and practiced in Part II of this book. Read the text again, paying attention to all the pronouns.

EXERCISE
16·4

List the prepositions and words that include prepositions in Text II.

_____

_____

_____

_____

*Categorize the prepositions and words that include prepositions into inseparable prepositions or separate prepositions, and indicate whether the preposition is combined with attachable pronouns, **dharf zaman** (adverb of time), **dharf makan** (adverb of place), and with interrogative articles.*

EXAMPLE

اشتريت الجريدة مبم محل بجانب الجامعة واشتريت مجلة أيضاً.

separate preposition: من

inseparable preposition combined with a dharf makan: بجانب

separate preposition compound with an attached pronoun: منه

١ _____

٢ _____

٣ _____

٤ _____

٥ _____

٦ _____

٧ _____

٨ _____

٩ _____

١٠ _____

١١ _____

١٢ _____

١٣ _____

١٤ _____

١٥ _____

١٦ _____

١٧ _____

١٨ _____

١٩ _____

٢٥ _____

٢١ _____

٢٢ _____

٢٣ _____

٢٤ _____

_____ ٢٥

_____ ٢٦

_____ ٢٧

_____ ٢٨

_____ ٢٩

_____ ٣٠

_____ ٣١

Translate Text II into English.

_____

_____

_____

_____

_____

_____

_____

_____

_____

_____

_____

_____

_____

_____

_____

_____

_____

_____

_____

_____

_____

Answer key

I♦ PRONOUNS

1 Subject pronouns

1·1

I am Algerian (s. m.). ١
I am Iraqi (s. f.). ٢
We are Syrians (pl. m.). ٣
We are Egyptians (pl. f.). ٤
You are Moroccan (s. m.). ٥
You are Emirati (s. f.). ٦

You are Saudis (d. m.). ٧
You are Yemenis (d. f.). ٨
You are Tunisians (pl. m.). ٩
You are Jordanians (pl. f.). ١٠
He is Bahraini (s. m.). ١١
She is Qatari (s. f.). ١٢

They are Sudanese (d. m.). ١٣
They are Palestinians (d. f.). ١٤
They are Libyans (pl. m.). ١٥
They are Kuwaitis (pl. f.). ١٦

1·2

١ أنا طالب.
٢ أنا دكتورة.
٣ نحن مهندسون.
٤ نحن ممرضات.
٥ أنتَ صديق.
٦ أنتِ زميلة.

٧ أنتما مصريان.
٨ أنتما مغربيتان.
٩ أنتم في الصف.
١٠ أنتن مدرسات.
١١ هو سوري.
١٢ هي أردنية.

١٣ هما لبنانيان.
١٤ هما موظفتان.
١٥ هم في المكتبة.
١٦ هن في الحديقة.

1·3

١ أنا أكتب رسالة
٢ نحن نحب مشاهدة الأفلام القديمة.
٣ أنتَ تكتب وظيفتَك.
٤ أنتِ تقرئين الدرس.
٥ أنتما تزوران أصدقاءكما.
٦ أنتم تعرفون عدة لغات.
٧ أنتن تستمعن إلى الموسيقى.
٨ هم يسكنون في هذا البيت.

٩ هو يشتري الجريدة.
١٠ هي تتذكر أصدقاء طفولتها.
١١ هما يحبان أختهما الصغيرة.
١٢ هما تحترمان والديهما.
١٣ هم يجلسون في المقهى.
١٤ هن يسهرن في النادي.
١٥ أنتم ستفتتحون الاجتماع يا سيادة الرئيس.

		1.4
١ نحن أصدقاء.	٦ أنتما فتاتان.	١١ هما رجلان.
٢ هي طالبة.	٧ أنتم إخوة.	١٢ هما امرأتان.
٣ أنتَ والد.	٨ أنتن أخوات.	١٣ هم أعمام.
٤ أنتِ والدة.	٩ أنا هنا.	١٤ هن خالات.
٥ أنتما والدان.	١٠ هوهناك.	

1.5

١ تستمع إلى الموسيقى العربية.

She listens to Arabic music.

٢ أنتما أخوان وتسكنان في بيت كبير.

You are two brothers and you live in a big house.

٣ نعمل في مصنع السيارات.

We work in a car factory.

٤ يشاهد المباريات الرياضية على التلفاز.

He watches sports on TV.

٥ هل أنتَ الطالب الجديد؟ وهل تدرس العربية؟

Are you the new student? Do you study Arabic?

٦ هما صديقتان قديمتان وتزوران بيتنا كل أسبوع.

They are two old friends and they visit our house every week.

٧ تطبخين لزوجك وأولادك يوم الجمعة.

You cook for your husband and children on Friday.

٨ يساعدن والدتهن في عمل البيت.

They help their mother with housework.

٩ تعتنين بأولادكن كثيراً.

You take so much care of your children.

١٠ هما طالبان في السنة الثالثة وسوف يتخرجان السنة القادمة.

They are two third-year students and they will graduate next year.

١١ تحبون مساعدة كل جيرانكم.

You like to help all your neighbors.

١٢ أحب قراءة الروايات العاطفية.

I like to read romantic novels.

١٣ يكتبون رسائل إلى أصدقائهم في عيد الميلاد.

They write letters to their friends on Christmas.

١٤ أنتما زميلان، وتعملان في نفس الشركة.

You are colleagues and you work in the same company.

١ هو كلب ضخم وجميل.

It is a large and beautiful dog.

٢ هي عظيمة مثل كل أفكاره.

It is great like all of his ideas.

٣ هي أكلت اللحم.

It ate the meat.

٤ هي في الشوارع.

They are in the streets.

٥ هي في البيوت.

They are in the houses.

٦ هو على الطاولة الجديدة.

It is on the new table.

٧ هي على الكرسي.

It is on the chair.

٨ هي في المكتبة.

They are in the library.

٩ هو قريب من النهر.

It is close to the river.

١٠ هو بعيد عن الجامعة.

It is far from the university.

١١ هي جميلة وجديدة.

It is beautiful and new.

١٢ هي نامت على الأريكة.

It slept on the sofa.

١٣ هو يحب الأولاد.

It likes the kids.

١٤ هي ممتعة وأنا أحب قراءتها في العطلة.

They are entertaining and I love reading them on vacations.

١٥ هي جميلة وأنا أحب الجلوس فيها.

They are beautiful and I like sitting in them.

2 Possessive pronouns

2·1

١ مكتبك قريب و مكتبي بعيد.

Your office is close by and my office is far.

٢ حديقتي جميلة ولكن حديقته أجمل.

My garden is beautiful but his garden is more beautiful.

٣ بابنا من الخشب و بابكم من الحديد.

Our door is (made of) wood and your door is (made of) iron.

٤ زوجك مهندس و زوجها طبيب.

Your husband is an engineer and her husband is a doctor.

٥ والدتهن في العمل و والدتكن في البيت.

Their mother is at work and your mother is at home.

٦ بيتكم في المدينة و بيتهم في الريف.

Your house is in the city and their house is in the countryside.

٧ أولادهما في البيت و أولادكما في الملعب.

Their kids are at home and your kids are in the playground.

٨ سيارتكم حمراء و سيارتنا زرقاء.

Your car is red and our car is blue.

٩ أسرتها صغيرة و أسرتِك كبيرة.

Her family is small and your family is big.

١٠ عملكم سهل و عملهن صعب.

You work is easy and their work is difficult.

١١ غرفتكماصغيرة و غرفتهما واسعة.

Your room is small and their room is spacious.

١٢ مدرستها في شمال المدينة و مدرستك في الجنوب.

Her school is in the north of the city and your school is in the south.

2·2

١٦ لونهما
Their color

١١ سيارته
His car

٦ مكتبتها
Its library

١ كتابه
His book

١٧ حديقتهم
Their garden

١٢ طاولتها
Her table

٧ ألعابهم
Their toys

٢ مكتبها
Her office

١٨ نكرياتها
Its memories

١٣ بابه
Its door

٨ بيته
His house

٣ بيتهم
Their house

١٩ أسماؤهن
Their names

١٤ أصواتها
Their sounds

٩ قلمها
Her pen

٤ لونها
Its color

٢٠ غرفتهما
Their room

١٥ صورهن
Their photos

١٠ زوجته
His wife

٥ احترامهما
Their respect

2·3

١٣ حديقتهم
Their garden

١٠ أستاذها
Her teacher

٧ مدرستكم
Your school

٤ عائلتك
Your family

١ كتابي
My book

١٤ أختهن
Their sister

١١ جامعتهما (d. m.)
Their university

٨ مدينتكن
Your city

٥ صديقكما (d. m.)
Your friend

٢ بيتنا
Our house

١٥ جلالتكم
Your majesty

١٢ سيارتهما (d. f.)
Their car

٩ طفله
His child

٦ جاركما (d. f.)
Your neighbor

٣ دراجتك
Your bicycle

2·4

١ I love my family.

٢ Our house is near the river.

٣ Your friend George is kind.

٤ Your book is new, my dear Samira.

٥ I told Sa'id and Su'ad, "Your mother is very smart."

٦ We told Maha and Muna, "Your father is rich."

٧ Your teacher is in the office.

٨ Your university is famous.

٩ His car is old.

١٠ Her bicycle is new.

١١ I have two friends, Fu'ad and Khalid, and their sister is called Laila.

١٢ My two (female) friends are Hana' and Sana', and their brother's name is Samir.

١٣ Their neighbor is kind.

١٤ Their school is near their house.

١٥ I want to meet you, your majesty.

2·5

١١ غرفة نومهما
Their bedroom

٦ صديقة طفولتكما
Your childhood (female) friend

١ ساعة يدي
My (hand) watch

١٢ طاولة مطبخهما
Their kitchen table

٧ فناجين قهوتكم
Your coffee cups

٢ شباك غرفتنا
Our room's window

١٣ أغطية سريره
His bedcovers

٨ علبة بريدهن
Their mailbox

٣ عنوان بيتكَ
Your home address

١٤ رقم هاتفكن
Your telephone number

٩ باب مكتبه
His office door

٤ غطاء طاولتكِ
Your table cloth

١٠ غطاء رأسها
Her head cover

٥ إبريق شايكما
Your tea pot

2·6

My outstanding (female) students ١	Your elementary school ٨
Our dear paternal and maternal aunts ٢	His little son ٩
Your loving grandmother ٣	Her new students ١٠
My favorite uncle ٤	Their only daughter ١١
Your little child ٥	Their old (female) friend ١٢
Your beautiful garden ٦	Their old address ١٣
Your elder sister ٧	Their kind mother ١٤

2·7

The director's table and chair ١	The cat's head and tail ٦
The neighbor's house and garden ٢	The director's assistant and secretary ٧
The child's father and mother ٣	The students' books and notebooks ٨
Our neighbor's wife and daughter ٤	The room's door and window ٩
The beginning and the end of the year ٥	The writer's novels and short stories ١٠

2·8

١ جاء أبوه وأمه إلى اجتماع الآباء في مدرستنا.
٢ أنت صديقي ومثل أخي.
٣ هل زاركم أخوكم؟
٤ أبونا يحبنا كثيراً.
٥ أخوك صديقي
٦ قرأ أبوها الجريدة.
٧ أين أبوك؟
٨ كتب أخوهن الرسالة.
٩ أبوكما أستاذ في الجامعة.
١٠ أمهم في البيت، وأبوهم في العمل.
١١ أخوكن طالب في الجامعة.
١٢ أبوهما رجل طيب.
١٣ حدثنا أخوكما عن رحلته إلى بغداد.
١٤ قابلت أخاك أمس.
١٥ أعطت أخاها الكتاب.
١٦ أحب أبي كثيراً.
١٧ أعرف أمه وأباه.
١٨ هل أخبرتم أخاكم؟
١٩ نحترم أبانا كثيراً.

٢٠ شاهدنا أخاهم في الحفلة.
٢١ زرت أخاك في مكتبه.
٢٢ يساعدن أباهن في العناية بالحديقة.
٢٣ انتظرنا أباكن في المحطة.
٢٤ أنا درست أخاهما في الجامعة.
٢٥ ستسافر مع أخيها.
٢٦ جاء مع أبيه وأمه إلى الحفلة.
٢٧ صديقي يسكن مع أخيك.
٢٨ سافر مع أبي وأخي.
٢٩ سيتكلم المدير مع أبيكم.
٣٠ قدمن الهدية إلى أخينا في عيد ميلاده.
٣١ ستقضي العيد مع أمها وأبيها.
٣٢ استمعنا إلى أخيك وهو يغني في الحفلة.
٣٣ اتصلن بأبيهن عند وصولهن.
٣٤ تعرفت على أبيكما منذ سنة.
٣٥ أخي يلعب كرة القدم مع أخيهم.
٣٦ أخي يدرس مع أخيكن.
٣٧ هذا الموظف يعمل في مكتب أبيهما.

2·9

١ معلموك	٧ زائراكن	١٣ معلمَيك	١٩ زائرَيكن
٢ طفلاهما	٨ مشاهدوها	١٤ طفليَهما	٢٠ مشاهدَيها
٣ مساعدونا	٩ جاراكما	١٥ مساعدَينا	٢١ جارَيكم
٤ والداكم	١٠ قائلوه	١٦ والدَيكم	٢٢ قائلَيه
٥ مديروهن	١١ سكرتيرتاهم	١٧ مدربَيهن	٢٣ سكرتيرتيهم
٦ زميلتاك	١٢ نائباي	١٨ زميلتَيك	٢٤ نائبَيّ

١ الشركة ومديرها

The company and its manager

٢ كتاب اللغة العربية الجديد وصفحاته

The new book of Arabic language and its pages

٣ مكتبات الجامعة وكتبها

The libraries of the university and their books

٤ البيوت وأبوابها

The houses and their doors

٥ الموسيقى الكلاسيكية ونغماتها

Classical music and its tunes

٦ النوافذ وستائرها

The windows and their curtains

٧ الجامعة القديمة وطلابها

The old university and its students

٨ الغرفة وأثاثها

The room and its furniture

٩ المكاتب وموظفوها

The offices and their employees

١٠ القلم وحبره

The pen and its ink

١١ البحر وأمواجه

The sea and its waves

١٢ الأقفال ومفاتيحها

The locks and their keys

١٣ طاولة العشاء الجديدة وغطاؤها الملون الجديد

The new dinner table and its new colorful cloth

١٤ المدرسة الابتدائية وأساتذتها المتخصصون في اللغة العربية

The elementary school and its teachers who specialize in Arabic language

١٥ القمر وضوؤه

The moon and its light

١٦ الشمس وأشعتها

The sun and its beams

١٧ النجوم وأنوارها

The stars and their lights

١٨ المدن الكبيرة وسكانها المشغولون بالعمل دائماً

The big cities and their inhabitants who are always busy at work

١٩ الفصول وتنوعها

The seasons and their variations

٢٠ الربيع وجماله

Spring and its beauty

٢١ الشتاء ومطره

Winter and its rain

٢٢ القهوة العربية بالهال ونكهتها

The Arabic coffee with cardamom and its flavor

٢٣ الأنهار وضفافها

The rivers and their banks

٢٤ الورود الدمشقية العطرة وألوانها

The fragrant Damascene roses and their colors

٢٥ شجرة الياسمين وعطرها

The jasmine tree and its fragrance

3 Object pronouns

3·1

١ هو صديقنا وهو يحبنا كثيراً.

He is our friend and he likes us very much.

٢ هو صديقكَ وهو يحبكَ كثيراً.

He is your friend and he likes you very much.

٣ هو صديقكِ وهو يحبكِ كثيراً.

He is your friend and he likes you very much.

٤ هو صديقكما وهو يحبكما كثيراً (d. m.).

He is your friend and he likes you very much.

٥ هو صديقكما وهو يحبكما كثيراً (d. f.).

He is your friend and he likes you very much.

٦ هو صديقكم وهو يحبكم كثيراً.

He is your friend and he likes you very much.

٧ هو صديقكن وهو يحبكن كثيراً.

He is your friend and he likes you very much.

٨ هو صديقه وهو يحبه كثيراً.

He is his friend and he likes him very much.

٩ هو صديقها وهو يحبها كثيراً.

He is her friend and he likes her very much.

١٠ هو صديقهما وهو يحبهما كثيراً.

He is their friend and he likes them very much.

١١ هو صديقهم وهو يحبهم كثيراً.

He is their friend and he likes them very much.

١٢ هو صديقهن وهو يحبهن كثيراً.

He is their friend and he likes them very much.

3·2

١ قرأه في عطلة عيد الميلاد.

He read it during Christmas vacation.

٢ اشترتها من المكتبة.

She bought it from the library.

٣ غسلتها بعد العشاء.

She washed them after dinner.

٤ شاهدناه الليلة الماضية.

We watched it last night.

٥ وضعناها حول المائدة.

We put them around the table.

٦ تناولناها في الصباح.

We drank it in the morning.

٧ سأضعها في المزهرية.

I will put them in the vase.

٨ اشترتها من السوق.

She bought them from the market.

٩ طبخته لهما.

She cooked it for them.

١٠ تناولاهما في الكافيتريا.

They had them at the cafeteria.

3.3

١ زملائي يحترمونني كثيراً.
My friends respect me very much.

٢ يزوروننا كل أحد.
They visit us every Sunday.

٣ أنا أحبكَ كثيراً ياأبي.
I love you very much, Dad!

٤ سنقابلكِ في المقهى يا أمي.
We will meet you in the café, Mom!

٥ نحن لا نعرفكِما.
We do not know you.

٦ رأيتكما في الطريق.
I saw you on the street.

٧ سنزوركم غداً.
We will visit you tomorrow.

٨ أنتن طالبات ذكيات وأنا أحترمكن.
You are smart students and I respect you.

٩ كلمته بالهاتف.
I talked to him on the phone.

١٠ حدثها عن السفر إلى القاهرة.
He told her about traveling to Cairo.

١١ هما جاران لطيفان وأنا أحبهما.
They are (two) kind neighbors and I like them.

١٢ هما صديقتان قديمتان وأنا أعرفهما جيداً.
They are (two) old (female) friends and I know them very well.

١٣ أنا أحب أصدقائي وأساعدهم.
I love my friends and help them.

١٤ اتصلتْ ببناتها وأخبرتهن عن الحفلة.
She called her daughters and told them about the party.

١٥ نلقاكم قريباً يا سمو الأمير.
We will see you soon your highness.

3.4

١٧ رفعوه	١٣ يسعدونهم	٩ يساعدهم	٥ يدرسها	١ أعرفها
١٨ غسلتها	١٤ أغمضهما	١٠ كتبهما	٦ قابلناها	٢ تناولتها
١٩ سندعوهم	١٥ قابلتهن	١١ أحبهن	٧ اشتراها	٣ زاروه
٢٠ ألقتها	١٦ لمحته	١٢ تشبهينها	٨ تحترمهما	٤ قرأته

3.5

١ سمعناها هذا المساء في النادي.
We heard it today at the club.

٢ أخبرته أنني سأذهب إلى المكتبة.
I told him that I was going to the library.

٣ سافر إلى بيروت ليقابلهم.
He traveled to Beirut to meet them.

٤ سألها عن موضوع المحاضرة.
He asked her about the topic of the lecture.

٥ أنا ذاهبة هذا الصباح لأقابله.
I am going to meet him this morning.

٦ حفظت كل الكلمات الجديدة قبل أن أحضره.
I memorized all the new words before I attended it.

٧ يا محمد! هل ستذهب يوم الجمعة لتزورهما؟
Are you going to visit them on Friday, Muhammad?

٨ شاهدناه في السينما يوم السبت الماضي.
We watched it in the cinema last Saturday.

٩ اشتريتها من المكتبة الجديدة.
I bought them from the new bookstore.

١٠ قرأته السنة الماضية.

I read it last year.

١١ أعطيتهن كتبي القديمة.

I gave them my old books.

١٢ زرعتها في حديقتي.

I planted them in my garden.

١٣ ساعدها في كتابة الوظيفة.

He helped her write the assignment.

١٤ أخذهم إلى المطعم الصيني.

He took them to the Chinese restaurant.

١٥ قرأتها المدرسة في الصف.

The teacher read them in the class.

١٦ حدثتهم عن رحلتي إلى المغرب.

I told them about my trip to Morocco.

١٧ وضعتها في الحقيبة.

I put them in the bag.

١٨ سيدعوهم لتناول القهوه معه.

He will invite them to have coffee with him.

١٩ هل رأيتموهما واقفتين أمام باب بيتهما؟

Have you seen them standing in front of the door of their house?

3.6

٦ هل قابلت أستاذ الأدب العربي الجديد؟
هل قابلته؟

٧ سألنا الموظفات عن العنوان.
سألناهن عن العنوان.

٨ سيدعو جيرانه الجدد إلى حفلة عيد الميلاد.
سيدعوهم إلى حفلة عيد الميلاد.

٩ صنعت كعكة لخطيبها في عيد الحب.
صنعتها لخطيبها في عيد الحب.

١٠ لا توقظ الأطفال، من فضلك.
لا توقظهم، من فضلك.

١ سأزور صديقي القديم يوم الجمعة.
سأزوره يوم الجمعة.

٢ شاهدوا الفيلم في نادي الجامعة.
شاهدوه في نادي الجامعة.

٣ هل تعرف كيف تكتب اسمك بالعربية؟
هل تعرف كيف تكتبه بالعربية؟

٤ اشترى بعض الورود الحمراء لحبيبته في عيد ميلادها.
اشتراها لحبيبته في عيد ميلادها.

٥ يحب زملاءه وطلابه، وهم يحبونه كثيراً.
يحبهم وهم يحبونه كثيراً.

4   Prepositional pronouns

4.1

٥ أخوه يسكن قريباً من أسرتي وهو أيضا يسكن قريبا منّا.

٦ جلست مع صديقي على الأريكة وجلست أخته بيننا.

٧ لا تذهبوا دوننا إلى الحفلة.

٨ لديه موعد مع الطبيب.

١ وضعت ثقتي فيه ووضع ثقته فيَّ.

٢ استعرنا دفاترهم واستعاروا بعض الكتب منّا.

٣ نسكن بعيداً عن الجامعة والمكتبة أيضا بعيدة جداً عنّا.

٤ زرنا أصدقاءهم وسألنا عنهم وزاروا أصدقاءنا وسألوهم عنّا.

4·2

١٣ نظرت إليه.

١٤ جاء إلينا أمس.

١٥ هو يشير إليكِ يا صديقتي.

١٦ سنزور كل الأصدقاء الذين نحلم أن نسافر إليهم.

١٧ أرسل إليَّ وروداً بيضاء.

١٨ ذهبوا إليكما بالسيارة.

١٩ أهدى إليهما ألعابا جميلة.

٢٠ قدموا إليك بعض الاقتراحات.

٢١ سنعود إليكن يا أخواتي.

٢٢ اشتاق إليها.

٢٣ استمع إليكم لساعات.

٢٤ حملوا إليهن خبراً ساراً.

١ والدكم يعتمد عليكم كثيراً.

٢ هذان هما الكرسيان اللذان يجلسان عليهما.

٣ فرض عليكن بعض الواجبات.

٤ هطل المطر علينا.

٥ يهبط الليل عليك فجأة.

٦ شباكنا يطل عليهم.

٧ شعرنا بالقلق عليكما.

٨ طلب منها البقاء ولم يجبرها عليه.

٩ أغلق عليَّ الباب.

١٠ حرموا عليهن السفر وحيدات.

١١ اقترحوا عليك بعض الحلول.

١٢ نثروا الزهور عليهما.

4·3

١٠ عندها قطة وكلب.

She has a cat and a dog.

١١ عندكن أفكار عظيمة.

You have great ideas.

١٢ هل لك أصدقاء في الجامعة؟

Do you have friends at the university?

١٣ معه كومبيوتر في السيارة.

He has a computer with him in the car.

١٤ إنها تمطر، هل معك مظلة؟

It is raining, do you have an umbrella?

١٥ ليس عنده تلفاز ولكن عنده راديو.

He does not have a television but he has a radio.

١٦ أضعت قلمي. هل معك قلم؟

I lost my pen. Do you have a pen?

١٧ كانت له حبيبة والآن هو وحيد.

He used to have a girlfriend and now he is lonely.

١ معها كتاب في الحقيبة.

She has a book in the bag.

٢ له صديق في طرابلس.

He has a friend in Tripoli.

٣ عندهم بيت واسع.

They have a spacious house.

٤ هل عندكما محاضرات هذا المساء؟

Do you have lectures this evening?

٥ هل لكم كثير من الأصدقاء؟

Do you have many friends?

٦ عندهما شركة تجارية.

They have a commercial company.

٧ لها أربعة إخوة.

She has four brothers.

٨ معي دولار في جيبي.

I have one dollar in my pocket.

٩ لهن خال في أمريكا.

They have a maternal uncle in America.

١ ذهبت إلى المكتبة لكتابة مقالة عنه.

I went to the library to write an article about him.

٢ اشتريت كتابي من المكتبة التي كنت قد ذهبت إليها مرة معهم.

I bought my book from the library where I had gone once with them.

٣ سأذهب بعد الغداء لأتمشى فيها.

I will go to walk in it after lunch.

٤ هل تعرف أن صديقنا سيقضي عيد الميلاد معهما؟

Do you know that our friend will spend Christmas with them?

٥ لها سبعة أخوة.

She has seven brothers.

٦ عنده بيت كبير وحديقة واسعة.

He has a big house and a spacious garden.

٧ لديها بيت في الريف.

They have a house in the countryside.

٨ اشتريت صحيفة ومجلة منه.

I bought a newspaper and a magazine from it.

٩ مشينا الأسبوع الماضي إليها وجلسنا فيها حتى المساء.

We walked to it last week and sat in it until the evening.

١٠ كتبت وظيفة اللغة العربية به.

I wrote the assignment of the Arabic language with it.

١١ عندما انتقلنا إلى بيتنا الجديد أقمنا حفلة لنتعرف عليهم.

When we moved to our new house we threw a party to get to know them.

١٢ معظم أصدقائي العرب يجلسون فيه.

Most of my Arab friends sit in it.

٨ عليكم حفظ الكلمات الجديدة.

You have to memorize the new words.

٩ عليه كتابة الوظيفة.

He has to write the homework.

١٠ عليها كتابة التمارين.

She has to write the exercises.

١١ عليكن زيارة جدتكن.

You have to visit your grandmother.

١٢ عليهم أخذ خالتهم إلى الطبيب.

They have to take their maternal aunt to the doctor.

١٣ عليَّ شراء هدية لصديقي.

I have to buy a present for my friend.

١٤ عليهن مساعدة أسرتهن في الإعداد للحفلة.

They have to help their family prepare for the party.

١ عليَّ الدراسة قبل الامتحان.

I have to study before the exam.

٢ علينا الذهاب إلى السوق لشراء الطعام.

We have to go to the market to buy food.

٣ عليكم احترام والديكم.

You have to respect your parents.

٤ عليهما قراءة صحف اليوم.

They have to read today's newspapers.

٥ عليك تنظيف البيت.

You have to clean the house.

٦ عليك غسل الصحون.

You have to wash the dishes.

٧ عليكما التفكير في المستقبل.

You have to think about the future.

١ اليوم امتحان اللغة العربية في الجامعة.

اليوم امتحان اللغة العربية فيها.

٢ يذهب الطلاب الساعة التاسعة صباحا إلى مكتبة الجامعة.

يذهب الطلاب الساعة التاسعة صباحا إليها.

٣ يدخل الطلاب إلى قاعة الامتحان الساعة العاشرة.

يدخل الطلاب إليها الساعة العاشرة.

٤ يجلس الطلاب على المقاعد الخشبية.

يجلس الطلاب عليها.

٥ يضعون كتبهم في حقائبهم.

يضعون كتبهم فيها.

٦ يكتبون أسماءهم بأقلامهم.

يكتبون أسماءهم بها.

٧ يخرج الأستاذ دفتر الأسماء من حقيبته.

يخرج الأستاذ دفتر الأسماء منها.

٨ يقرأ الأستاذ أسماء الطلاب في دفتره.

يقرأ الأستاذ أسماء الطلاب فيه.

٩ يعطي الأستاذ أوراق الامتحان للطلاب.

يعطي الأستاذ أوراق الامتحان لهم.

١٠ يجيب الطلاب على الأسئلة.

يجيب الطلاب عليها.

١١ عندما ينتهون يضعون كل الأوراق أمام الأستاذ.

عندما ينتهون يضعون كل الأوراق أمامه.

١٢ يغادر الطلاب قاعة الامتحان الساعة الواحدة.

يخرج الطلاب الساعة الواحدة.

١٣ يمشون، ثم يدخلون المقهى العربي مع أصدقائهم.

يمشون، ثم يدخلون المقهى العربي معهم.

١٤ يتناولون القهوة العربية، ويتحدثون عن الامتحان.

يتناولون القهوة العربية، ويتحدثون عنه.

5   Pronouns and other particles

5·1

١ The (female) students are in the university library.

٢ They behave as if they are at home.

٣ He opened the letter and read it but he did not understand it.

٤ The two students are Egyptians from the city of Alexandria.

٥ They might tell her.

٦ The two (female) students are Syrian from the city of Tartous.

٧ I feel that you are a real friend.

٨ I wish they'd understand.

٩ The students are in the classroom.

١٠ I know that you are traveling tomorrow.

١١ The street is wide.

١٢ We waited but they didn't come.

١٣ Nobody can carry out the task except you.

١٤ The day passed quickly, as if it was only an hour.

١٥ Wait, they might be coming.

١٦ The library is open until seven o'clock in the evening.

١٧ Everybody attended except you.

١٨ We invited family and friends, and nobody attended except them.

١٩ If only you were here.

٢٠ The child is beautiful. He looks like an angel when he smiles.

5·2

١ سأذهب إلى الكافيتيريا لعلهم يجلسون هناك.

I will go to the cafeteria, perhaps they are sitting there.

٢ قالت لنا إنّه سيؤجل اجتماع اليوم إلى الأسبوع القادم.

She told us that he would postpone today's meeting until next week.

٣ قرعنا على بابكم هذا الصباح ولكنها لم تكن في البيت.

We knocked at your door this morning but she was not there.

٤ الغرفة باردة ... كأنها صفر هنا.

The room is cold . . . as if it is zero degrees here.

٥ أعرف أنك تحبني وأنهم مثل أهلي.

I know that you love me and that they are like my family.

٦ لم أتعرف على أي طالب سواهما.

I did not get to know any students except them.

٧ أحتاج لبعض المساعدة في نقل كتبي إلى غرفتي الجديدة ولكنهن مشغولات.

I need some help to move my books to my new room but they are busy.

٨ إنهم سيأخذون إجازات أطول هذه السنة.

They will take longer vacations this year.

٩ ليته يعطينا وظائف أسهل.

If only he'd give us easier homework.

١٠ لم يحضر الفيلم في النادي أحد سواهم.

Nobody attended the film at the club except them.

5·3

١ فهموا أنه كان سعيداً باللقاء.

٢ قرأنا في الصحف أنهم يواجهون صعوبات في الوصول لاتفاق.

٣ قرأت الرسالة ولكنّ هذا لايعني أنها سترسل جوابا.

٤ لم يتصوروا أنك ستوافق.

٥ هل تعتقد أنّ الوضع سيتغير؟

٦ هي تشعر أنه يحاول الاقتراب منها.

٧ هم افترضوا أنها سوف تعود.

٨ عرفت أنه يريد تغيير عمله.

٩ تذكرت أنه قد وعد أن يفعل ذلك.

١٠ قالوا إنك ستحل المشكلة أخيراً.

١١ لم يعلم أنّ الامتحانات قد تأجلت بسبب الثلج.

١٢ أحست أنه يريد أن يتعرف عليها.

5·4

١ قال لهم إنهما سعيدان.

٢ قالت لك إنها ستسافر لزيارة أقاربها.

٣ قال لي إنه يحب أن يساعد زملاءه في واجباتهم.

٤ سيقولان له إنهما سيزوران جدتهما يوم الأحد.

٥ قالوا لنا إنهم كانوا يدرسون في المكتبة القريبة من جامعتهم.

٦ قالتا لها إنهما صديقتان منذ الطفولة وتسكنان في نفس الحي.

٧ سنقول لهم إننا نرغب في زيارة كل الأماكن التي قرأنا عنها في الكتب.

٨ قالت لهما إنها البنت الوحيدة في الصف ومعها خمسة طلاب.

٩ قلن لي إنهن طالبات اللغة العربية ولكنهن يدرسن التاريخ ولغات أخرى.

١٠ سيقول لهم إنه سيتصل بخطيبته مها لأنهما سيسافران معا إلى دمشق والقاهرة وسيأخذان معهما بعض الهدايا لأصدقائهما.

6 Demonstrative pronouns

6·1

١ هذا الأستاذ يدرس اللغة العربية.
This teacher teaches Arabic language.

٢ هذه الأستاذة تسكن في لندن.
This (female) teacher lives in London.

٣ هؤلاء الأطباء يعملون في المشفى.
These doctors work in the hospital.

٤ هذان الكتابان على الطاولة.
These two books are on the table.

٥ وضعت هذين الكتابين في الحقيبة.
I put these two books on the table.

٦ هاتان المجلتان على الرف.
These two magazines are on the shelf.

٧ قرأت هاتين المجلتين.
I read these two magazines.

٨ هذه الكتب من المكتبة.
These books are from the library.

٩ اشتريت هذه المجلات أمس.
I bought these magazines yesterday.

6·2

١ استمتعت بتلك القصة.
I enjoyed that story.

٢ نحب أولئك الجيران.
We love those neighbors.

٣ جلسنا في ذلك المقهى.
We sat in that café.

٤ تانك الأستاذتان تدرسان العربية.
Those two teachers teach Arabic.

٥ تعرفنا على ذينك الزميلين الجديدين.
We got to know those two new (male) colleagues.

٦ حدثها عن تلك الخطة وعن ذلك القرار.
He told her about that plan and that decision.

٧ ذهبوا إلى تلك الحديقة العامة.
They went to that public park.

٨ تلك السيارات غالية.
Those cars are expensive.

٩ خرج من ذلك الباب.
He left out of that door.

١٠ قرأت تينك المجلتين.
I read those two magazines.

١١ ذانك الكتابان ممتعان.
Those two books are enjoyable.

١٢ تلك الأفلام قديمة.
Those films are old.

١٣ تلك المدن بعيدة.
Those cities are far.

6·3

١ هذا باص.

٢ هذه سيارة صغيرة.

٣ هذا الباص كبير.

٤ هذه السيارة الصغيرة جديدة.

٥ هذا ولد.

٦ هذه بنت.

٧ هذا الولد سعيد.

٨ هذه البنت جميلة.

٩ هذا الولد الصغير سعيد.

١٠ هذه البنت الصغيرة جميلة.

١١ هؤلاء أولاد سعداء.

١٢ هؤلاء بنات جميلات جداً.

١٣ هؤلاء الأولاد سعداء جداً.

١٤ هؤلاء البنات جميلات جداً.

١٥ هؤلاء الأولاد الصغار سعداء جداً.

١٦ هؤلاء البنات الصغيرات جميلات جداً.

<table>
<tr>
<td>

١٠ هؤلاء هم طلاب السنة الثالثة.

These are the students of the third year.

١١ هؤلاء هن طالبات السنة الأولى.

These are the (female) students of the first year.

١٢ هؤلاء هم مدراء الجامعات الخاصة.

These are the directors of the private universities.

١٣ هذان هما الأستاذان الجديدان.

These are the two new teachers.

١٤ هاتان هما السكرتيرتان اللطيفتان.

These are the two kind secretaries.

١٥ هذا هو المطعم الشامي.

This is the Shami (Levantine) restaurant.

١٦ هذه هي الأطباق اللذيذة.

These are the delicious dishes.

١٧ تلك هي المشروبيات الباردة.

Those are the cold drinks.

١٨ هذه هي طاولتنا المفضلة.

This is our favorite table.

</td>
<td>

6.4

</td>
</tr>
</table>

١ هذه هي المدينة القديمة.

This is the old city

٢ هؤلاء هم الأطفال السعداء.

These are the happy children.

٣ تلك هي دفاتر الولد وأقلامه.

Those are the boy's notebooks and pens.

٤ هذه هي ثياب البنت وألعابها.

These are the girl's clothes and toys.

٥ هذا هو النادي الجامعي.

This is the university club.

٦ تلك هي حديقة الجامعة.

That is the university park.

٧ هذه هي أشجار الياسمين.

These are the Jasmine trees.

٨ ذلك هو الكتاب الجديد.

That is the new book.

٩ هذا هو وزير التعليم.

This is the education minister.

6.5

١ هذا فيلم جميل، ومع هذا لن أشاهده لأن عندي وظيفة.

This is a beautiful film but in spite of that I will not watch it because I have homework.

٢ الطقس بارد، ولهذا لن أذهب إلى الحديقة.

The weather is cold and for that reason I am not going to the park.

٣ كان متعباً، ومع ذلك لعب كرة القدم مع أصدقائه.

He was tired, nevertheless, he played football with his friends.

٤ هو صديقي وأنت كذلك صديقتي.

He is my friend and you are my friend as well.

٥ عندي امتحان غداً، ولذلك سأدرس طوال الليل.

I have an exam tomorrow so I will study throughout the night.

٦ سنتناول الغداء وبعد هذا سنتناول القهوة.

We will have lunch and then coffee.

٧ سيذهبون إلى المكتبة وبعد ذلك سيذهبون إلى المقهى.

They will go to the library and then to the café.

7 Relative pronouns

7·1

١ البيت الذي يقع قرب النهر جميل جداً.
The house that is located near the river is very beautiful.

٢ الحديقة التي تحيط بالبيت جميلة جداً.
The garden that surrounds the house is very beautiful.

٣ الرجل الذي يسكن في هذا البيت صديقي.
The man who lives in this house in my friend.

٤ العجوزان اللذان يسكنان معه هما والداه.
The two old people who live with him are his parents.

٥ السيدتان اللتان تزورانهم أحياناً هما خالتاه.
The two ladies who visit them sometimes are his maternal aunts.

٦ المرأة التي تزورهم كل يوم هي أخته.
The woman who visits them every day is his sister.

٧ والأطفال الذين يقضون معهم يوم الأحد هم أولاد أخته.
And the children who spend Sundays with them are his sister's children.

٨ زرت صديقي ووالديه اللذين يسكنان معه.
I visited my friend and his parents who live with him.

٩ وتعرفت على خالتيه اللتين تزورانه أحياناً.
And I got to know his maternal aunts who visit him sometimes.

7·2

١ هذه هي المقالة التي قرأتها.
This is the article that you read.

٢ هذه هي القصة التي استمتعت بها.
This is the story that I enjoyed.

٣ هؤلاء هم الأصدقاء الذين سافرنا معهم.
These are the friends that we traveled with.

٤ هذه هي الموظفة التي اتصلنا بها.
This is the (female) employee that we called.

٥ هذا هو المطعم الذي تغدينا فيه.
This is the restaurant where we had lunch.

٦ هذا هو الثوب الذي اشترته.
This is the dress that she bought.

٧ هذا هو الأستاذ الذي أعجبت به.
This is the teacher that she admired.

٨ هذه هي الأشجار التي مشينا بينها.
These are the trees that we walked among.

٩ هذه هي المظلة التي جلسنا تحتها.
This is the umbrella that we sat under.

١٠ هذا هو النهر الذي سبحتم فيه.
This is the river that you swam in.

١١ هذه هي البحيرة التي لعبوا حولها.
This is the lake that they played around.

١٢ هذا هو الجسر الذي عبروه.
This is the bridge that they crossed.

١٣ هذه هي الموسيقى التي استمعنا إليها.
This is the music that we listened to.

١٤ هذا هو القلم الذي كتبنا به.
This is the pen that we wrote with.

7.3

١ سمير هو الزميل الذي أعمل معه.

٢ زرنا عائلة ✓ تسكن في قريتنا.

٣ السيارة التي تقف أمام باب بيته هي سيارة والده.

٤ هذه هي الشركة التي يعمل بها.

٥ هذا هو الكتاب الذي يتكون من ١٤ فصلاً.

٦ هذا أذكى شاب ✓ قابلته في حياتي.

٧ تلقيت هدية ✓ فرحت بها كثيراً.

٨ هذه هي الجامعة التي ندرس بها.

٩ هذا أسعد يوم ✓ عشته في حياتي.

١٠ سأزور هذا الصيف أصدقائي الذين يدرسون في جامعة حلب.

١١ قابلت البنت التي تدعى سلمى.

١٢ سقى ورودا زرعها ✓ في الحديقة.

١٣ سمعت كلاماً ✓ أسعدني.

١٤ قابل في الحفلة امرأة ✓ أعجب بها.

١٥ سأزور مدينة تدمر لأرى معبد بعل الذي رأينا صوره في كتاب التاريخ.

١٦ "علاء الدين" فيلم مشهور ✓ أنتجته شركة ديزني.

7.4

١ هذه هي المقالة المهمة التي حدثتك عنها أمس.

٢ تعرفنا في مدينة تدمر على السياح الذين جاؤوا لزيارة معبد بعل.

٣ هو الصديق الذي أتكلم معه عن مشاكلي وأحلامي.

٤ حدثنا عن الفيلم الذي شاهده في نادي الجامعة.

٥ دعت الموظفتين اللتين تعملان معها في نفس المكتب إلى الحفلة.

٦ أرسلت بطاقات إلكترونية في رأس السنة للطالبات اللواتي درسن معي في الجامعة.

٧ أهداني صديقي الكتاب الذي كنت أتمنى دوما الحصول عليه.

٨ هذه هي الرواية الممتعة التي يمكن أن تعجب كل من يقرأها.

٩ اشترينا البيت الذي كنا نحلم به دوماً ونتمنى أن نسكنه.

١٠ زرنا المطعم الذي قدم لنا أطباقا عربية لذيذة.

١١ هؤلاء هم الأصدقاء الذين سافرنا معهم إلى سوريا الشهر الماضي.

١٢ التقيت في الشارع البنت التي تسكن عائلتها البيت المقابل لبيت أهلي وسلمت عليها.

7.5

١ كل من يعرفها يحبها.

٢ هي تعرف كل ما يفكر به.

٣ لا أعرف ما تعنيه هذه الكلمة بالعربية.

٤ يريد أن يحدثها عن كل ما يشعر به.

٥ سنقول له ما يرغب بسماعه.

٦ على من يريد أن يتعلم عن الثقافة العربية أن يعيش في بلد عربي.

٧ لا أعرف من تابع دراسته من زملائي، أو من وجد وظيفة.

7.6

١ حدثته عن كل اللوحات التي رأيتها في المعرض.

حدثته عن كل ما رأيته في المعرض.

٢ أخبرونا عن كل الطلاب الذين التقوا بهم في الحفلة.

أخبرونا عن كل من التقوا بهم في الحفلة.

٣ أخبر أمه عن كل القصص التي قرأها في درس الأدب العربي.

أخبر أمه عن كل ما قرأه في درس الأدب العربي.

٤ أخبرت صديقاتها عن كل الأخبار التي سمعتها في السوق.

أخبرت صديقاتها عن كل ما سمعته في السوق.

٥ هم يحترمون كل الناس الذين يحترمونهم.

هم يحترمون كل من يحترمهم.

٦ أخبر زملاءه عن كل البلدان التي قرر زيارتها في المستقبل.

أخبر زملاءه عن كل ما قرر زيارته في المستقبل.

٧ أعلنت الجامعة أنها ستعطي منحاً لكل الطلاب الفقراء الذين يحتاجون إليها.

أعلنت الجامعة أنها ستعطي منحا لكل من يحتاج إليها.

٨ هل سترسل في عيد الميلاد بطاقات لكل الزملاء الذين يعملون معك في الشركة.

هل سترسل في عيد الميلاد بطاقات لكل من يعمل معك في الشركة.

٩ هي تتذكر جيداً كل الروايات التي قرأتها في طفولتها.

هي تتذكر جيدا كل ما قرأته في طفولتها.

١٠ إذا توقفت الآن عن دراسة اللغة العربية فسوف تنسى معظم الكلمات التي تعلمتها.

إذا توقفت الآن عن دراسة اللغة العربية فسوف تنسى معظم ما تعلمته.

١١ وضعت في حقيبتي كل الثياب التي سآخذها معي في رحلتي.

وضعت في حقيبتي كل ما سآخذه معي في رحلتي.

١٢ زرت كل الأصدقاء الذين درست معهم في المدرسة الثانوية.

زرت كل من درست معهم في المدرسة الثانوية.

8   Interrogative pronouns

8·1

٦ ماذا ستفعل يوم الجمعة؟

What will you do on Friday?

٧ ماذا أكلوا في المطعم؟

What did they eat in the restaurant?

٨ أنت حزين! ما المشكلة؟

You are upset! What is the problem?

٩ ماذا فعلت أمس؟

What did you do yesterday?

١٠ ماذا قرأت في العطلة؟

What did you read during the holiday?

١ ما هذه الضجة؟

What is this noise?

٢ ماذا يعمل والدك؟

What does your father do?

٣ ماذا تدرس في الجامعة؟

What do you study at the university?

٤ ما اسم صديقك؟

What is the name of your friend?

٥ ما لون سيارتك؟

What is the color of your car?

8·2

١ متى سيبدأ الفيلم؟

When will the film start?

The film will start in ten minutes.

٢ من الذي اتصل بك؟

Who called you?

A colleague who works with me in the office.

٣ كيف تعلمت اللغة العربية؟

How did you learn Arabic?

I learned its grammar in the university first, then I learned conversation in Arab countries.

٤ أين تسكن عائلتك؟

Where does your family live?

My father and mother live in London, and my brother works in Dubai.

٥ أيّ سيارة سيارتك؟

Which car is your car?

That small red car.

٦ من أخبرك بالقصة؟

Who told you about the story?

The secretary.

٧ ماذا اشتريت من السوق؟

What did you buy from the market?

Some fruits and vegetables.

٨ متى ستزور جدتك؟

When are you going to visit your grandmother?

Next week.

٩ أين مكتب المدير؟

Where is the office of the director?

On the second floor.

١٠ من صاحب هذا المحل؟

Who is the owner of this store?

My cousin.

١١ ما هذا الصوت؟

What is this sound?

This is our neighbor singing.

١٢ كيف كان الامتحان؟

How was the exam?

Very difficult.

8·3

١ مع من ستسافر إلى بيروت؟

With whom are you traveling to Beirut?

With my brother and some friends.

٢ في أي جامعة درست العربية؟

At which university did you study Arabic?

At the university of Damascus.

٣ من أين صديقك؟

Where is your friend from?

His father is Egyptian and his mother is British.

٤ لماذا لم تحضر المحاضرة اليوم؟

Why didn't you attend the lecture today?

I was out of town visiting my family.

٥ بكم اشتريت المجلة الأدبية؟

How much did you buy the literary magazine for?

Twenty liras.

٦ إلى أين يذهب هذا القطار؟

Where is this train going?

To Baghdad.

٧ إلى متى ستبقى في حلب؟

Until when are you staying in Aleppo?

Until the end of the holiday.

٨ لماذا عدت من النادي مبكراً؟

Why did (you) come early from the club?

Because some friends will visit me.

٩ من أين اشتريت هذه السجادة الجميلة؟

Where did you buy this beautiful rug?

From an Iranian shop in the old market.

١٠ في أي مكان سنلتقي؟

Where are we going to meet?

At the park.

١١ مع من كنت تتكلم على الهاتف؟

With whom were you speaking on the phone?

With the director of the company in which I am going to work.

١٢ إلى أين سنذهب بعد الامتحان؟

Where are we going after the exam?

To the Arabic café in London.

8·4

١ لا، ليس عندنا امتحان غداً.

Do you have an exam tomorrow?

٢ نعم، أنا موظف في هذه الشركة.

Are you an employee in this company?

٣ نعم، هذه هي المكتبة التي تفتح يوم السبت.

Is this the library that opens on Saturday?

٤ لا، لم نر الفيلم الجديد.

Have you seen the new film?

٥ نعم، لي خال في أمريكا.

Do you have a maternal uncle in America?

٦ لا، لا أريدك أن تحضر لي شيئاً من السوق.

Do you want me to bring you anything from the market?

٧ نعم، سنحتاج لكل هذه الحقائب.

Are we going to need all these suitcases?

٨ نعم، هناك باص إلى شاطئ اللاذقية الجمعة عند منتصف الليل.

Is there a bus to the beach of Lattakia on Friday midnight?

٩ لا، ليس معنا بطاقات للمسرح.

Do you have tickets for the theater?

١٠ نعم، من الممكن تعلم لغتين في نفس الوقت.

Is it possible to learn two languages at the same time?

١١ لا، لم اتصل بصديقي الذي تخرج أمس.

Did you call your friend who graduated yesterday?

١٢ نعم، أنا متأكد أنهم سيصلون غداً.

Are you sure that they will arrive tomorrow?

٧ هل تحبين/تحب الحلويات العربية؟

٨ هل أرسلتَ/أرسلتِ بطاقات لأصدقائك في عيد الميلاد؟

٩ هل ستقيم عائلتكَ/عائلتكِ حفلة بعد تخرجك من الجامعة؟

١٠ هل لكَ/لكِ أصدقاء في العالم العربي؟

١١ هل هناك استراحة بعد هذا الدرس؟

١٢ هل تحب/تحبين أن تتناول القهوة معي؟

١ هل تعرفون من هو المدير الجديد؟

٢ هل عندكم سيارة أخرى؟

٣ هل هذه هي الصحيفة التي نشرت الخبر؟

٤ هل من الضروري ترجمة هذا السؤال؟

٥ هل تعرفون أين حديقة الجامعة؟

٦ هل معكَ/معكِ رقم هاتف المكتب؟

9 Nonhuman third person neutral pronoun

١ الحر سيشتد في الصيف.
It will get hotter in summer.

٢ الثلج ينزل على الجبال.
It is snowing over the mountains.

٣ الوقت مبكر جداً؛ لا يوجد أحد في المطعم.
It is very early; there is nobody in the restaurant.

٤ هذه فكرة جيدة وهي ذكية أيضاً.
This is a good idea and it is clever as well.

٥ هذا اقتراح عظيم وهو اقتراح جديد أيضاً.
This is a great suggestion and it is a new suggestion too.

٦ قطتي اسمها فلة وهي قطة جميلة.
My cat is called Fulla and it is a beautiful cat.

٧ كلبي اسمه بوبي وهو كلب ذكي.
My dog is called Bobby and it is a smart dog.

٨ الجو غائم اليوم وسينزل المطر طوال الليل.
It is very cloudy today and it will rain throughout the night.

٥ من المهم التحضير لدرس الأدب.

٦ من الواضح أنه يريد أن يدعوها إلى حفلته.

٧ ليس من المهم شراء الكتاب لأننا نستطيع أن نستعيره من المكتبة.

١ من الضروري شراء بعض الهدايا.

٢ ليس مناسباً الحديث عن المشكلة الآن.

٣ من الممكن الدراسة في المكتبة يوم السبت.

٤ من السهل إيجاد البيت إذا كان معك العنوان.

٧ عندما أعطاني الوردة وضعتها في كتابي.

٨ هذا هو فيلمي المفضل وأنا شاهدته عدة مرات.

٩ المعطف جميل ولكنه غال.

١٠ حديقتك مليئة بالماء والزهور. كأنها جنة صغيرة.

١١ مد السجادة وجلس عليها.

١٢ أحب بيتنا لأنه جميل وواسع.

١ سيارتي جديدة ولونها أحمر.

٢ بيتي أبيض وبابه بني.

٣ النافذة مفتوحة وزجاجها نظيف جداً.

٤ الكتاب قديم وغلافه قديم أيضاً.

٥ هذه هي المجلة العربية. اشتريتها أمس.

٦ أعطاني الكتاب لأقرأه خلال العطلة.

10 Practicing pronouns in context

اتصل بي اليوم صديقي أيمن الذي يدرس معي في المدرسة الابتدائية وقال "تبدو سعيداًجداً، لماذا؟"

قلت له: "لأننا مسافرون".

قال: "إلى أين؟"

قلت له: "أنا الآن مشغول، سأكتب لك رسالة إلكترونية بعد قليل".

قال: "ومتى ستعودون؟"

قلت: "لا أعرف". بعد دقائق كتبت له هذه الرسالة وأرسلتها بالبريد الإلكتروني:

"أنا سعيد جداً هذا الصباح ... بدأت اليوم عطلة أبي الصيفية ... ستسافر عائلتي إلى مدينة طرطوس غداً لقضاء أسبوعين في المدينة وعلى شاطئها كما نفعل كل سنة. خرج أبي باكراً ليحجز تذاكر سفرنا ... وضعت أمي في حقيبتنا الكبيرة ملابسي وملابس أخوتي الصيفية وثياب سباحتنا وألعابنا المائية و آلات تصويرنا بالإضافة إلى كل ما اشتراه أبي للعطلة.

طرطوس مدينة فينيقية جميلة واسمها الفينيقي "أرادوس". والبحر في تلك المدينة جميل وأمواجه زرقاء. أنا وأخوتي ووالدي نقضي يومنا عادة في السباحة وبناء بيوت على رمله بينما تتناول أمي قهوتها تحت المظلة وهي تنظر إلينا.

كلنا نحب السمك ولذلك نقضي وقت الغداء في المطاعم الجبلية أو في جزيرة أرواد حيث نتناوله ونحن نستمتع بالطبيعة هناك.

في المساء ننزل إلى المدينة ونتمشى في شوارعها أو نزور أقاربنا وكل من يدعونا من أصدقاء والدي. ونخرج معهم أحياناً إلى المطاعم والمقاهي".

٢٣ ـي possessive pronoun my mother	١٢ متى interrogative pronoun when	١ ـي prepositional pronoun he got in touch with me/he called me
٢٤ ـنا possessive pronoun our suitcase	١٣ ـه prepositional pronoun to him	٢ ـي possessive pronoun my friend
٢٥ ـي possessive pronoun my clothes	١٤ هذه demonstrative article this	٣ الذي relative pronouns who
٢٦ ـي possessive pronoun my siblings'	١٥ ـها object pronoun I sent it	٤ ـي prepositional pronoun with me
٢٧ ـنا possessive pronoun our swimming suits	١٦ أنا subject pronoun I	٥ لماذا؟ interrogative pronoun why?
٢٨ ـنا possessive pronoun our toys	١٧ هذا demonstrative article this	٦ ـه prepositional pronoun to him
٢٩ ـنا possessive pronoun our cameras	١٨ ـي possessive pronoun my father's	٧ ـنا pronoun with other particles because we (are)
٣٠ ـما relative pronoun what, whatever	١٩ ـي possessive pronoun my family	٨ إلى أين interrogative pronoun where to?
٣١ ـه object pronouns he bought it	٢٠ ـها possessive pronoun its beach	٩ ـه prepositional pronoun to him
٣٢ ـي possessive pronoun my father	٢١ ـي possessive pronoun my father	١٠ أنا subject pronoun I
٣٣ ـها possessive pronoun its name	٢٢ ـنا possessive pronoun our travel	١١ ـك prepositional pronoun to you

٣٤ تلك demonstrative article — that	٤١ ـي possessive pronoun — my mother	٤٨ نحن subject pronoun — we
٣٥ ـه possessive pronoun — its waves	٤٢ ـها possessive pronoun — her coffee	٤٩ ها possessive pronoun — its streets
٣٦ أنا subject pronoun — I	٤٣ هي subject pronoun — she	٥٠ ـنا possessive pronoun — our relatives
٣٧ ـي possessive pronoun — my siblings	٤٤ ـنا prepositional pronoun — to us	٥١ من relative pronoun — who, whoever
٣٨ ي possessive pronoun — my father	٤٥ ـنا possessive pronoun — all of us	٥٢ نا object pronoun — invites us
٣٩ ـنا possessive pronoun — our day	٤٦ ـ preposition + demonstrative article — therefore	٥٣ ي possessive pronoun — my father
٤٠ ـه possessive pronoun — its sand	٤٧ ـه object pronoun — we have/eat/take it	٥٤ ـهم prepositional pronoun — with them

10.2 هذا هو الطالب الذي التقيت به الشهر الماضي. أصبحنا صديقين لأنه لطيف جداً، ولأنه مثلي يدرس اللغة العربية في جامعة دمشق. هو يحب اللغة العربية، ويتحدث بها بطلاقة مع أصدقائه العرب. سافرت معه الأسبوع الماضي إلى حلب ويعلبك، وزرته أمس في بيته الذي يقع في المدينة القديمة. عرفني على صديقه الذي يسكن قريباً منه، والذي يدرس العربية أيضاً.

Feminine third person singular هـي:

هذه هي الطالبة التي التقيت بها الشهر الماضي. أصبحنا صديقين لأنها لطيفة جداً، ولأنها مثلي تدرس اللغة العربية في جامعة دمشق، وهي تحب اللغة العربية وتتحدث بها بطلاقة مع أصدقائها العرب. سافرت معها الأسبوع الماضي إلى حلب ويعلبك، وزرتها أمس في بيتها الذي يقع في المدينة القديمة. عرفتني على صديقها الذي يسكن قريباً منها، والذي يدرس العربية أيضاً.

Masculine third person dual هم:

هذان هما الطالبان اللذين التقيت بهما الشهر الماضي. أصبحنا أصدقاء لأنهما لطيفان جداً، ولأنهما مثلي يدرسان اللغة العربية في جامعة دمشق، وهما يحبان اللغة العربية ويتحدثان بها بطلاقة مع أصدقائهما العرب. سافرت معهما الأسبوع الماضي إلى حلب ويعلبك، وزرتهما أمس في بيتهما الذي يقع في المدينة القديمة. عرفاني على صديقهما الذي يسكن قريباً منهما، والذي يدرس العربية أيضاً.

Feminine third person dual هما:

هاتان هما الطالبتان اللتان التقيت بهما الشهر الماضي. أصبحنا أصدقاء لأنهما لطيفتان جداً، ولأنهما مثلي تدرسان اللغة العربية في جامعة دمشق، وهما تحبان اللغة العربية وتتحدثان بها بطلاقة مع أصدقائهما العرب. سافرت معهما الأسبوع الماضي إلى حلب ويعلبك، وزرتهما أمس في بيتهما الذي يقع في المدينة القديمة. عرفتاني على صديقهما الذي يسكن قريباً منهما، والذي يدرس العربية أيضاً.

Masculine third person plural هـم:

هؤلاء هم الطلاب الذين التقيت بهم الشهر الماضي. أصبحنا أصدقاء لأنهم لطيفون جداً، ولأنهم مثلي يدرسون اللغة العربية في جامعة دمشق، وهم يحبون اللغة العربية، ويتحدثون بها بطلاقة مع أصدقائهم العرب. سافرت معهم الأسبوع الماضي إلى حلب ويعلبك، وزرتهم أمس في بيتهم الذي يقع في المدينة القديمة. عرفوني على صديقهم الذي يسكن قريباً منهم، والذي يدرس العربية أيضاً.

Feminine third person plural هنّ:

هؤلاء هن الطالبات اللواتي التقيت بهن الشهر الماضي، أصبحن أصدقاء لأنهن لطيفات جداً، ولأنهن مثلي يدرسن اللغة العربية في جامعة دمشق، وهن يحببن اللغة العربية، ويتحدثن بها بطلاقة مع أصدقائهن العرب. سافرت معهن الأسبوع الماضي إلى حلب وبعلبك، وزرتهن أمس في بيتهن الذي يقع في المدينة القديمة. عرفنني على صديقهن الذي يسكن قريباً منهن، والذي يدرس العربية أيضاً.

 PREPOSITIONS

11 Inseparable prepositions

11·1

١ وضع النقود بجيبه.
He put the money in his pocket.

٢ كيف يمكنك أن تصادق شخصا كهذا!
How could you befriend a person like that!

٣ سافر بالقطار من القاهرة لأسوان.
He traveled by train from Cairo to Aswan.

٤ ذهبنا للمقهى يوم الجمعة.
We went to the café on Friday.

٥ ذهبا للسينما لمشاهدة الفيلم.
They went to the cinema to watch the film.

٦ كلمته من المطار بهاتفها الجوال.
She called him from the airport from her mobile phone.

٧ نمنا يوم الأحد للساعة العاشرة.
We slept until ten o'clock on Sunday.

٨ بكم اشتريت خاتمك الذهبي؟
How much did you buy your golden ring for?

٩ تالله لأنجح في الامتحان.
I swear to God that I will succeed in the exam.

١٠ الفتاة جميلة كالوردة.
The girl is pretty like a rose.

١١ هو قوي كالنمر.
He is strong like a tiger.

١٢ اشتريت حقيبة جديدة بألف ليرة.
I bought a new bag for a thousand liras.

١٣ وضع صورتها بإطار.
He put her photo in a frame.

١٤ هذا الرجل يمشي كراعي البقر.
This man walks like a cowboy.

١٥ أخبرت أصدقائي بالهاتف.
I told my friends on the phone.

١٦ قدم الوظيفة للأستاذ.
He submitted the homework to the teacher.

١٧ يركض كالحصان.
He runs like a horse.

١٨ تالله لآخذ حقي.
I swear to God that I will take my right.

١٩ مشيت لبيت أصدقائي.
I walked to my friends' house.

٢٠ أفضل السفر بالقطار على السفر بالباص.
I prefer traveling by train to traveling by bus.

٢١ الغرفة باردة كالثلاجة.
The room is cold like a refrigerator.

٢٢ بقيت للمساء في البيت.
I stayed at home until the evening.

٢٣ سأذهب إلى مكتبة الجامعة لكتابة البحث.
I will go to the university library to write a research.

٢٤ الصديق الوفي كالأخ.
A faithful friend is like a brother.

٢٥ ذهب لمكتبه بالسيارة.
He went to his office by car.

11.2

١١ مروا بي وخذوني معكم إذا قررتم الخروج.

١٢ ما بهم؟ لقد تغيروا كثيراً.

١٣ طرح عليها حلا لكنها لم ترض به.

١٤ يحبان أطفالهم كثيراً، ويهتمان بهم.

١٥ هل تذكرون عندما التقيت بكم لأول مرة في المكتبة.

١٦ يحب السفر إلى البلدان البعيدة التي يحلم بها أحياناً.

١٧ هذا هو المقهى الذي تعارفنا به.

١٨ نحن أقوياء فلا تستهينوا بنا.

١٩ تذكرت كل التجارب التي مررت بها خلال هذه السنوات.

٢٠ سأرسل في العيد رسائل لأساتذتي الذين أحبهم، أوسأتصل بهم.

١ هذا هو القلم الذي كتبت به الرسالة.

٢ استقبل الوزير الضيوف ورحب بهم.

٣ شرحت لهما الموضوع وأقنعتهما به.

٤ يحترم الحب ويؤمن به.

٥ ويحترم الصداقة، ولكنه لا يؤمن بها.

٦ لا يحبك، ولكنه معجب بك.

٧ سأريك بعض صور طفولتي التي أحتفظ بها.

٨ وثقت بهن، وحكت لهن عن مشكلتها.

٩ هم معجبون بوالديهم، ويحاولون أن يقتدوا بهما.

١٠ قدموا وعودا كثيرة لكنهم لم يلتزموا بها.

11.3

١ تكلمت معه بالعربية فلم يفهموا ما قالته له.
She talked to him in Arabic so they did not understand what she said to him.

٢ توفي والدهن، وترك لهن مالاً كثيراً.
Their father died and left them lots of money.

٣ لن أطلب منكم المساعدة إلا إذا احتجت لها.
I will not ask you for help unless I need it.

٤ كنت أمشي في الشارع حين ظهر لي فجأة.
I was walking on the street when he suddenly appeared.

٥ هؤلاء هم أصدقاؤك المخلصون فاغفر لهم إذا أخطؤوا أحياناً.
These are your sincere friends so forgive them if they make mistakes sometimes.

٦ أشتاق لكم كثيراً يا أحبابي.
I miss you a lot my loved ones.

٧ انظر إلى الكاميرا وابتسم لها.
Look at the camera and smile into it.

٨ اعترفت لهن أنها وقعت في حب زميلها.
She confessed to them that she has fallen in love with her colleague.

٩ أرسل لي صور قريتك الجميلة.
Send me the pictures of your beautiful village.

١٠ سنقدم لكما اقتراحاً عظيماً عندما نلقاكما.
We will provide you a great suggestion when we meet you.

١١ تركت لك على طاولة المطبخ البقلاوة التي تحبها.
I left the baklava you love on the kitchen table for you.

١٢ لا يحب استعمال السيارة إلا إذا اضطر لها.
He does not like to use the car unless he is forced to.

١٣ قابلنا وعبر لنا عن قلقه من الموضوع.
He met us and expressed his concern about the subject to us.

١٤ لمح لهما عن خطته عدة مرات عندما التقاهما.
He hinted to them about his plan several times when he met them.

١٥ عندما سيلقاها سيهمس لها بكلمات الحب.
When he sees her, he will whisper words of love in her ears.

١٦ سمعنا أنك ستعزف على العود في المقهى فجئنا لنستمع لك.

We heard that you will play the lute at the café so we came to listen to you.

١٧ لم أسمع أخباركن منذ زمن. ماذا حدث لكن يا صديقاتي؟

I didn't hear your news (haven't heard from you) for a while. What happened to you my friends?

١٨ سأزورهم غداً لأنني اشتقت لهم كثيراً.

I will visit them tomorrow because I miss them very much.

١٩ أخبروني كل ما حدث لكم منذ سافرتم.

Tell me about everything that happened to you since you traveled.

٢٠ عندما مرت التاكسي لوح لها فتوقفت.

When the taxi passed he waved to it so it stopped.

٢١ سيعطي حبيبته الهدايا التي اشتراها لها.

He will give his girlfriend the presents that he bought for her.

12 Separate prepositions

12·1

١ هو مختلف عن بقية أصدقائه.

٢ في الصباح يشرب الإنكليز الشاي مع الحليب، أما الفرنسيون فيشربون القهوة دون حليب.

٣ نسي القاموس في المكتبة.

٤ اشتريت من السوق القديم ركوة قهوة.

٥ استلقى على السرير وأخذ يفكر.

٦ مشينا معاً حتى المحطة.

٧ أدرس في البيت أحياناً، ولكنني أفضل الدراسة في المكتبة.

٨ عاد من العمل مبكراً اليوم.

٩ سيسافر غداً إلى السعودية.

١٠ قضيت عيد الميلاد مع أسرتي.

١١ وضع الكتاب على الرف.

١٢ تكلم في محاضرته عن الحقوق المدنية.

١٣ هل لدى المدير أية مواعيد اليوم؟

١٤ بيته يقع في وسط المدينة.

١٥ حضرت فيلماً وثائقياً عن الحرب العالمية الأولى.

١٦ شربنا قهوة في المقهى العربي.

١٧ وضعنا الصحون على طاولة الطعام.

١٨ انتظرناهم حتى المساء لكنهم لم يأتوا.

١٩ سيذهبان إلى المسرح يوم الأحد.

٢٠ لن يأتي إلى الحفلة دون/مع صديقته.

١ ما اسم الجامعة التي تخرج منها ابنك؟

٢ ذهب معها إلى المطار.

٣ هذه هي الغرفة التي أسكن فيها.

٤ منذ عودته من رحلة القاهرة لم يتوقف عن الحديث عنها.

٥ تعرفت في الرباط على أصدقاء جدد، وسافرت معهم إلى مراكش.

٦ سأذهب دونكم إذا كنتم لا تريدون الذهاب معي إلى الحفلة.

٧ لدينا اختبار في اللغة العربية غداً.

٨ اتصلنا بأسرتك وسألناها عنك.

٩ أعجب باللوحة والألوان التي استخدمت فيها.

١٠ سأقضي هذا المساء في المكتب لأن لدي عمل كثير.

١١ أعادوا لي المجلات التي أخذوها مني.

١٢ يتمنى أن يزور البيت الذي ولد فيه.

١٣ غضب منكما بسبب تصرفكما الغريب.

١٤ هذا هو الكتاب الذي حدثتك عنه.

١٥ هذا هو المدير الذي لأحب أن أعمل معه.

١٦ أقنعته بزيارة المدينة التي تعيش فيها.

١٧ لن أذهب دونك إلى أي مكان أبداً.

١٨ أرسلت بطاقات بريدية للأصدقائي الذين درست معهم في الجامعة.

١٩ أعادوا لنا الكتب التي أخذوها منا.

٢٠ اشترى حقيبة ووضع كتبه فيها.

٢١ زاروا أصدقاءنا وسألوهم عنا.

١ نظر إلي ولم يقل شيئاً.

He looked at me and did not say anything.

٢ انكسر الرف لأننا وضعنا القواميس الضخمة عليه.

The shelf broke because we put the large dictionaries on it.

٣ شعرت بالقلق عليهما.

I was worried about them.

٤ يتذكر كل الأماكن التي ذهب إليها في القاهرة.

He remembers all the places that he went to in Cairo.

٥ السلام عليكن أيتها الصديقات.

Al-salam 'alaykum (peace be upon you), (female) friends!

٦ أرسلت إليهما رسالة منذ شهر.

I sent them a letter a month ago.

٧ يجب علي الذهاب إلى المكتبة.

I must go to the library.

٨ أرسلوا إلينا بعض الهدايا.

They sent us some presents.

٩ عليكم أن تدرسوا للامتحان.

You have to study for the exam.

١٠ جاء إلينا من بعيد.

He came to us from afar.

١١ سيقدم إليك هدية.

He will offer you a present.

١٢ تعرفت عليهم في دمشق.

I got to know them in Damascus.

١٣ انظر إلي عندما أتحدث إليك.

Look at me when I talk to you.

١٤ أعادت إليه كل الهدايا والرسائل.

She returned all the presents and letters to him.

١٥ طلب كرسياً ليجلس عليه.

He asked for a chair to sit on.

١٦ أرسلت إليهم عدة رسائل.

I have sent several letters to them.

١٧ أنت صديقي وأنا اعتمد عليك.

You are my friend and I rely on you.

١٨ حدثتهم عن الوظيفة التي حصلت عليها.

She told them about the job she has got.

١٩ قدم إليهن نصيحة.

He offered them advice.

٢٠ جئنا إليكن بأخبار سعيدة.

We came to you with (we brought you) happy news.

13   Dharf

13·1

١ كنت أطبخ العشاء حين دخولك.

I was cooking dinner when you came in.

٢ تجمع الطلاب خارج القاعة.

The students gathered outside the hall.

٣ لدي اجتماع مهم الآن. سأراك بعد ساعة.

I have an important meeting now. I will see you in an hour.

٤ نام أثناء الفيلم.

He slept during the film.

٥ وقف الطفل خلف أمه.

The child stood behind his mother.

٦ أخفى شعوره تجاه صديقته.

He has hidden his feelings towards his (female) friend.

٧ من الرجل الواقف بين المدير والسكرتيرة؟

Who is the man standing between the director and the secretary?

٨ أوقف سيارته أمام باب المكتب.

He stopped his car in front of the office door.

٩ القطة نائمة تحت السرير.

The cat is sleeping under the bed.

١٥ جلسنا معاً حول الطاولة.

We sat together around the table.

١١ سأكتب الرسالة خلال الأسبوع القادم.

I will write the letter next week.

١٢ انتظر الطالب الأستاذ داخل المكتب.

The student waited for the teacher inside the office.

١٣ عند التقييم السنوي وضعه المدير في مرتبة دون مراتب زملائه في العمل.

In the annual review, the boss positioned him in a rank that is lower than that of his peers.

١٤ مشينا بسرعة نحو/تجاه المكتبة.

We walked quickly toward the library.

١٥ التفت صوب البحر.

He turned toward the sea.

١٦ نام طوال المحاضرة.

He slept throughout the lecture.

١٧ ركضنا تحت المطر عبر الشارع.

We ran under the rain across the street.

١٨ اجتمع الناس عند بوابة المعرض.

People gathered at the gate of the exhibition.

١٩ وضعنا الطاولة وسط الغرفة.

We put the table in the middle of the room.

٢٠ مشت القطة فوق السطح.

The cat walked over the roof.

٢١ نام ساعة قبل الغداء.

He slept for an hour before lunch.

٢٢ أوقف السيارة قدام البيت.

He stopped the car in front of the house.

٢٣ انتظرها مقابل الباب.

He waited for her at the door.

٢٤ انتظرناهم في المقهى عوض الانتظار في الشارع.

We waited for them at the café instead of waiting on the street.

٢٥ اجتمع الناس قبالة المعرض.

People gathered opposite to the exhibition.

١ كانت المحاضرة مملة فنام أثناءها.

٢ وقف الوالدان، ووقف الطفل خلفهما.

٣ جلسنا على الأريكة، وجلست القطة بيننا.

٤ عبر لها عن مشاعره تجاهها.

٥ تعرف عليها قبل سنتين، وكان حينها مايزال طالباً.

٦ ضعي الصورة أمامكِ على المكتب.

٧ أشعلنا المدفأة وجلسنا معاً حولها.

٨ لدي إجازة طويلة. سأسافر إلى عدة بلدان عربية خلالها.

٩ وضعت الكتاب على الطاولة، ووضعت الجريدة تحته.

١٠ وقفت أمام الباب بينما كان الأستاذ داخله.

١١ أنتما متكبران وتشعران أن كل الناس دونكما في الأهمية.

١٢ رأينا صديقنا فمشينا نحوه.

١٣ أغلقت السكرتيرة القاعة فتجمع الطلاب خارجها.

١٤ خرجت من الاجتماع بعدكن بدقيقة.

١٥ دخلنا الحديقة ومشينا عبرها.

١٦ هذا هو بيتنا، ومقابله بيت جدي.

١٧ كليتنا في آخر الشارع، وقبالتها تقع المكتبة.

١٨ رأوا الطائرات تحلق فوقهم.

١٩ ذهبوا إلى الحفلة قبلهن بساعة.

٢٠ وقف قدامنا وقرأ القصيدة.

٢١ أقامت الجدة حفلة واجتمعت العائلة عندها.

٢٢ وضعنا الصحون على الطاولة ووضعنا المزهرية في وسطها.

٢٣ التفت صوتي حين سمع صوتي.

١ ذهب إلى مكتب البريد بعد أن كتب الرسالة.

ذهب إلى مكتب البريد بعد كتابة الرسالة.

٢ شعرت الفتاة بالفرح حين رأت صديقها.

شعرت البنت بالفرح عند رؤية صديقها.

٣ سأزور صديقي بعد أن أتصل به.

سأزور صديقي بعد الاتصال به.

٤ لم نركم منذ زرناكم آخر مرة.

لم نركم منذ زيارتنا لكم آخر مرة.

٥ سأقرأ الكتاب قبل أن أسافر.

سأقرأ الكتاب قبل سفري.

٦ خرجوا من المكتبة بعد أن قرأوا كتبهم.

خرجوا من المكتبة بعد قراءة كتبهم.

٧ لم أتغيب عن أي محاضرة منذ عدت من سفري.

لم أتغيب عن أي محاضرة منذ العودة من سفري.

٨ بدأت حياتي حين تعرفت عليك.

بدأت حياتي حين التعرف عليك.

٩ سنذهب إلى المقهى قبل أن نشاهد الفيلم.

سنذهب إلى المقهى قبل مشاهدة الفيلم.

١٠ لم آخذ إجازة منذ بدأت العمل هنا.

لم آخذ إجازة منذ بدء العمل هنا.

١١ سأذهب إلى السوق بعد أن أنتهي من العمل.

سأذهب إلى السوق بعد الانتهاء من العمل.

١٢ هل أنهيتِ الكتاب قبل أن تنامي؟

هل أنهيتِ الكتاب قبل النوم؟

١ جلست بجواره أثناء المحاضرة.

٢ ساعدته في كتابة الوظيفة، وهو بالمقابل أصلح لها دراجتها.

٣ نشرب الشاي بدون حليب.

٤ خرج من بين الطلاب واحد وألقى خطاباً.

٥ خرج الرجل من تحت الخيمة.

٦ جلس في المقعد الأمامي وجلسنا في الخلف.

٧ عبر من أمامنا بصمت.

٨ مشى خطوتين إلى الأمام وخطوة إلى الوراء.

٩ وقع الفنجان من على الطاولة.

١٠ قفز من فوق السور.

١١ هو يقدم خدمات كثيرة لجيرانه بدون مقابل.

١٢ صاحب المكتبة صديقي، ولهذا أشتري كتبي من عنده.

١٣ في أعقاب الحرب صنعت أفلام كثيرة لتبرير ماحدث.

١٤ جلست في آخر صف بحيث أراه ولا يراني.

١ هذه فكرة جيدة، ولكنها خارجة عن الموضوع.

٢ إذا لم يكن عندك سيارة، فأنا أضع سيارتي تحت تصرفك.

٣ لا أستطيع مساعدتكم أبداً، فالموضوع خارج تماما عن إرادتي.

٤ لا أعرف هذا الطالب، ولم أقابله من قبل.

٥ أدونيس كاتب مشهور، وكتاباته معروفة حول العالم كله.

٦ نحن متأكدون أنه شخص طيب ويحب المساعدة وهو سيساعدك دون شك.

٧ هي تتفهم مشكلتكن وسوف تساعدكن على قدر طاقتها.

٨ أنا أختلف معك على بعض التفاصيل ولكني أتفق معك من حيث المبدأ.

٩ لا يمكن أن نتفق معهم أبداً لأننا نختلف معهم من حيث المبدأ.

١٠ هي تستخدم الإنترنت كثيراً. وقد تعرفت على صديقها من خلال إحدى مواقع الإنترنت.

١١ اكتشفوا كل أسرارهن من خلال قراءتهم لرسائلهن.

١٢ تفاءل فمازلت شاباً، والمستقبل كله أمامك.

١٣ عليكما أن تستعدا جيداً لأن أمامكما سنة من العمل الجاد.

١٤ أخوك الصغير هو الذي كسر المزهرية. كان يلعب في الغرفة، وأوقعها عن الطاولة أمام عيني.

١٥ لا تلتفت إلى الوراء. انس تلك التجربة، وضع الماضي كله وراءك.

14 Different functions of prepositional phrases

14·1

١ يتعامل مع جيرانه باحترام.
He deals with his neighbors respectfully.

٢ انتظروهم في المحطة بصبر.
They waited for them patiently at the station.

٣ كان متأخراً ولذلك مشى بسرعة.
He was late so he walked quickly.

٤ عاشوا في شقاء إلى أن وجد والدهم عملاً.
They lived in misery until their father found a job.

٥ هم على ما يرام ويرسلون تحياتهم.
They are very well and they send their greetings.

٦ قال لها وداعاً على أمل اللقاء ثانية.
He said goodbye to her in the hope of meeting again.

٧ كتب الجواب على منوال السؤال.
He wrote the answer in the same manner as the question.

٨ أنا على ثقة أنهم سيدرسون جيداً للامتحان.
I am sure they will study very well for the exam.

٩ غادرت البيت هذا الصباح على عجل.
I left home in a hurry this morning.

١٠ مشى على مهل يفكر في مستقبله.
He walked slowly thinking about his future.

١١ تعزف على البيانو وتغني بطريقة جميلة.
She plays the piano and sings beautifully.

١٢ ازداد عدد الطلاب هذه السنة بصورة ملحوظة.
The number of students increased remarkably this year.

١٣ أحب كل الألوان وأحب اللون الأزرق بصفة خاصة.
I love all colors but I love blue in particular.

١٤ ليس لدي صديق مفضل وأحب كل أصدقائي بشكل عام.
I do not have a favorite friend and I love all my friends in general.

١٥ يتكلم دائماً بهدوء.

He always speaks softly.

١٦ شعروا بالخوف عندما بدأ يتصرف بعنف.

They felt afraid when he started acting violently.

١٧ يحبون جدتهم لأنها تعاملهم بمحبة.

They love their grandmother because she treats them with love.

١٨ تابعوا النقاش باهتمام كبير.

They followed the discussion with great interest.

١٩ تكلم بصورة عامة ولم يقدم أية أمثلة.

He talked in general and did not give any examples.

٢٠ فهم معنى الكلمات اللاتينية بسهولة.

He easily understood the meaning of Latin words.

14·2
(The fronted predicate and **mubtada** have been shown for the first five answers for your guidance.)

١ في البداية تحية.

في البداية :fronted predicate

تحية :mubtada

A greeting at the beginning.

٢ فيها معهد.

فيها :fronted predicate

معهد :mubtada

It has an institute.

٣ لها تاريخ.

لها :fronted predicate

تاريخ :mubtada

It has a history.

٤ له سمعة.

له :fronted predicate

سمعة :mubtada

It has a reputation.

٥ للمعهد مبنى.

للمعهد :fronted predicate

مبنى :mubtada

The institute has a building.

٦ وراء المبنى حديقة.

There is a garden behind the building.

٧ حول النافورة طاولات.

There are tables around the fountain.

٨ وأمامه حديقة.

And there is a garden in front of it.

٩ في الطابق الأول من المبنى مكتب الاستقبال.

The reception office is on the first floor of the building.

١٠ على يسار مكتب الاستقبال غرفة الحاسوب.

The computer room is to the left of the reception office.

١١ في الطابق الثاني غرف الصف.

The classrooms are on the second floor.

١٢ وفي الطابق الثالث الكافيتيريا.

The cafeteria is on the third floor.

١٣ بين الكافيتيريا والمكتبة تليفون.

There is a phone between the cafeteria and the library.

١٤ في الكافيتيريا طاولات.

There are tables in the cafeteria.

١٥ على جدارها صور.

There are pictures on its wall.

١٦ في المزة معاهد.

There are institutes in Mezza.

١٧ في المعهد أساتذة.

There are teachers in the institute.

None. This sentence doesn't have a prepositional phrase. ١٨

١٩ خارج المبنى ضجيج.

There is noise outside the building.

٢٠ داخل المبنى هدوء.

There is calmness inside the building.

٢١ عند الظهر استراحة.

At midday/noon, there is a break.

٢٢ قبل الاستراحة درس.

Before the break there is a class.

٢٣ بعد الاستراحة درس.

After the break there is a class.

٢٤ فوق طاولتي رواية.

On my table there is a novel.

٢٥ بين صف القواعد وصف الأدب في المساء استراحة.

Between the grammar class and the literature class in the evening there is a break.

٢٦ تحت طاولتي حقيبة.

Under my table there is a bag.

٢٧ في دمشق الكثير من الأسواق.

There are plenty of markets in Damascus.

None. This sentence doesn't have a prepositional phrase. ٢٨

I will come back to my room shortly.

٢٩ في المساء حفلة.

There is a party in the evening.

٣٠ للجميع سلامي.

My greetings to everybody.

14·3

١ له أصدقاء

He has many friends in Egypt.

٢ عندنا امتحان

We have an exam in the Arabic language next week.

٣ معي كتب

I have many books (with me).

٤ لصديقتي عم

My friend has a paternal uncle in America.

٥ لها عم

My friend has a very rich paternal uncle in America.

٦ عندهم بيت

They have a beautiful house.

٧ معنا بعض الأصدقاء

We have some friends with us.

٨ لصديقي ثلاثة أخوة

My friend has three brothers (siblings).

٩ له ثلاثة أخوة

My friend has three brothers (siblings).

١٠ معك منديل؟

Your colleague has a cold. Do you have a tissue?

١١ عندك سيارة؟

Do you have a car?

14·4

١ ليس بعد الاستراحة درس في اللغة العربية.

٢ ليس فوق طاولتي رواية.

٣ ليس بين صف القواعد وصف الأدب في المساء استراحة/ليس هناك استراحة بين صف القواعد ...

٤ ليس تحت طاولتي حقيبة.

٥ ليس في المساء حفلة.

٦ ليس له أصدقاء كثيرون.

٧ ليس عندنا امتحان الأسبوع القادم.

٨ ليس معي كتب كثيرة.

٩ ليس لصديقتي أقارب يعملون في الخليج.

١٠ صديقتي ليس لها أقارب يعملون في الخليج.

١١ ليس لصديقي مساعد وسكرتيرة.

١٢ صديقي ليس له مساعد وسكرتيرة.

14·5

١ كان بعد الاستراحة درس.

ما كان بعد الاستراحة درس/لم يكن بعد الاستراحة درس.

٢ كانت فوق طاولتي رواية.

ماكان فوق طاولتي رواية/لم يكن فوق طاولتي رواية.

٣ كان بين صف القواعد وصف الأدب في المساء استراحة.

ما كان بين صف القواعد وصف الأدب في المساء استراحة. لم يكن بين صف القواعد وصف الأدب في المساء استراحة.

٤ كانت تحت طاولتي حقيبة.

ماكان تحت طاولتي حقيبة/لم يكن تحت طاولتي حقيبة.

٥ كانت في المساء حفلة.

ما كان في المساء حفلة/لم يكن في المساء حفلة.

٦ كان له أصدقاء كثيرون.

ما كان له أصدقاء كثيرون. لم يكن له أصدقاء كثيرون.

٧ كان عندنا امتحان الأسبوع القادم.

ما كان عندنا امتحان الأسبوع القادم/لم يكن عندنا امتحان الأسبوع القادم.

٨ كان معي كتب كثيرة.

ما كان معي كتب كثيرة/لم يكن معي كتب كثيرة.

٩ كان لصديقتي أقارب يعملون في الخليج.

ما كان لصديقتي أقارب يعملون في الخليج/لم يكن لصديقتي أقارب يعملون في الخليج.

١٠ صديقتي كان لها أقارب يعملون في الخليج.

صديقتي ما كان لها أقارب يعملون في الخليج/صديقتي لم يكن لها أقارب يعملون في الخليج.

١١ كان لصديقي مساعد وسكرتيرة.

ما كان لصديقي مساعد وسكرتيرة/لم يكن لصديقي مساعد وسكرتيرة.

١٢ صديقي كان له مساعد وسكرتيرة.

صديقي ما كان له مساعد وسكرتيرة/صديقي لم يكن له مساعد وسكرتيرة.

14·6

١ سيكون بعد الاستراحة درس/سيكون هناك درس بعد الاستراحة.

لن يكون بعد الاستراحة درس.

٢ سيكون هناك رواية فوق طاولتي.

لن يكون فوق طاولتي رواية/لن يكون هناك رواية فوق طاولتي.

٣ سيكون هناك بين صف القواعد وصف الأدب في المساء استراحة/ستكون استراحة ...

لن يكون بين صف القواعد وصف الأدب في المساء استراحة.

٤ سيكون تحت طاولتي حقيبة.

لن يكون تحت طاولتي حقيبة.

٥ سيكون في المساء حفلة.

لن يكون في المساء حفلة.

٦ سيكون له أصدقاء كثيرون.

لن يكون له أصدقاء كثيرون.

٧ سيكون عندنا امتحان الأسبوع القادم.

لن يكون عندنا امتحان الأسبوع القادم.

٨ سيكون معي كتب كثيرة.

لن يكون معي كتب كثيرة.

٩ سيكون لصديقتي أقارب يعملون في الخليج.

لن يكون لصديقتي أقارب يعملون في الخليج.

١٠ صديقتي سيكون لها أقارب يعملون في الخليج.

صديقتي لن يكون لها أقارب يعملون في الخليج.

١١ سيكون لصديقي مساعد وسكرتيرة.

لن يكون لصديقي مساعد وسكرتيرة.

١٢ صديقي سيكون له مساعد وسكرتيرة.

صديقي لن يكون له مساعد وسكرتيرة.

١ جلس إلى طاولته وأمامه أوراق الامتحانات كلها.

He sat at his table with all the exam papers in front of him.

٢ مشينا إلى المحطة ومعنا حقائبنا.

We walked to the station with our suitcases.

٣ دخلوا غرفة الاجتماع وفي رؤوسهم أسئلة كثيرة.

They entered the meeting room with many questions in their heads.

٤ جئت وفي نيتي أن أعتذر لكم.

I came here intending to apologize to you.

٥ غادر بلاده وبجيبه ألف ليرة فقط.

He left his country with only a thousand liras (pounds) in his pocket.

٦ رحل وفي قلبه سر كبير.

He departed with a big secret in his heart.

٧ نام وتحت مخدته صورتها.

He slept with her photo under his pillow.

٨ خرجوا من المطعم وعلى طاولتهم الكثير من الطعام.

They left the restaurant with lots of food on their table.

٩ جلس في المكتبة ومن حوله طلابه.

He sat in the library surrounded by his students.

١٠ بدأت العمل ولي من العمر عشرون سنة.

I started working when I was twenty years old.

١١ قطعوا الصحراء ووصلوا وعلى ثيابهم و وجوههم غبار.

They crossed the desert and arrived with dust on their clothes and faces.

١٢ يخططون لمستقبل ناجح ويتقدمون وفي عقولهم مشاريع كبيرة.

They are planning for a successful future and proceeding with big projects in their minds.

١٣ ذهبت إلى العمل وفي حقيبتي كل الأوراق.

I went to work with all the papers in my bag.

١٤ دخلنا البيت وعلى ثيابنا ومظلاتنا مياه المطر.

We entered the house with rainwater all over our clothes and umbrellas.

١٥ نام في الطريق وإلى جانبه كلبه.

He slept on the street with his dog by his side.

He came with the meeting papers. ١

He entered the room with his many suitcases. ٢

He brought us the happy news about home. ٣

He traveled to his country with one suitcase. ٤

He boarded the plane with two bags in his hands. ٥

He went to them with the news. ٦

He came with new stories. ٧

He arrived at his friend's birthday party with (bringing with him) his (female) friend ٨

14·9

١ قلنا لهم إننا سنزورهم غداً بعد أن ننتهي من العمل فقالوا، "أهلا بكن."

We told them that we were going to visit them tomorrow after we finish work and they said, "You are welcome!"

٢ قالت الأستاذة للطلاب عندما نجحوا في اختبار اللغة العربية، "مرحى لكم".

When the students succeeded in the test of the Arabic language the teacher said to them, "Bravo to you!"

٣ نحن سعداء بمجيئكم. مرحباً بكم وياً صدقائكم الأعزاء الذين جاؤوا معكم.

We are very happy that you came and welcome you and all your dear friends who came with you.

٤ عندما مر في الطريق رآهم جالسين أمام باب البيت فقال لهم، "السلام عليكم".

He saw them sitting in front of the house door when he passed through the street and he said to them, "Peace be upon you!"

٥ أنت مهندس عظيم! تحية لكَ ولكل من عملوا معك في هذا المشروع الناجح.

You are a great engineer! I salute you and all those who worked with you on this successful project.

٦ سأتصل بك غداً وأنت في طريقك إلى المطار لأقول لك مع السلامة.

I will call you tomorrow when you are on your way to the airport to say goodbye to you.

٧ عندما خرجت من البيت مشى والدي ورائي وهو يقول، "بأمان الله."

When I left the house, my father walked behind me saying, "With God's safety."

14·10

١ هن موريتانيات. هن من موريتانيا.

٨ هم صعيديون. هم من الصعيد.

٢ هما مراكشيان. هما من مراكش.

٩ أنتم كويتيون. أنتم من الكويت.

٣ نحن بحرينيات. نحن من البحرين.

١٠ هن يمنيات. هن من اليمن.

٤ هو مصري. هو من مصر.

١١ نحن سودانيات. نحن من السودان.

٥ أنا شامية. أنا من الشام.

١٢ هو قطري. هو من قطر.

٦ أنا إماراتي. أنا من الإمارات.

١٣ هما جزائريان. هما من الجزائر.

٧ هما أردنيتان. هما من الأردن.

١٤ أنا تونسي. أنا من تونس.

14·11

١ بغداد

The Baghdadi maqam is one of the ancient Arab musical arts developed at the hands of artists from the city of Baghdad.

٢ بيروت

Abu Al-Abd al-Bayruti is a popular fictional character of a witty narrator who lives in Beirut.

٣ تونس

The famous singer Ulayya al-Tunusiyya is one of the pioneers of popular Arabic songs and she is originally from Tunisia.

٤ حوران

The family of the famous thinker Albert Hawrani is spread all over Bilad al-Sham (Greater Syria). However, the family is originally from the valley of Hawran in south Syria.

٥ دمشق

Saint John Al-Taghlibi of Damascus worked as a minister under the Umayyad rule. He is originally from the tribe of Taghlib which lived around the Euphrates in Syria but his family is from Damascus.

٦ الرملة

The famous TV writer Linin al-Ramli is Egyptian but his grandfathers came from the city of Ramla in Palestine.

٧ الجزائر

The famous singer Warda al-Jaza'iriyya lived and became famous in Egypt, however, she is originally from Algeria.

٨ حلب

The Queen Nur al-Husayn is the wife of the late king of Jordan, King Husayn. Her maiden name is Nur al-Halabi. Her mother is American and her father is from the city of Aleppo in Syria.

٩ حمص

Deek al-Jinn al-Humsi is a well-known Arab poet. He was famous for his poems about his beloved, Ward. Deek al-Jinn lived all his life in the city of Hums.

١٠ البصرة

The famous scholar Hasan al-Bisri lived in the seventh century in the city of Basra in Iraq.

١١ الحجاز

The Hijazi family is spread over the two cities of Riyadh and Jedda. However, it originally came from Hijaz in Saudi Arabia.

١٢ انطاكية

Dawood Al-Antaki is a famous Syrian scholar who wrote books on medicine and astronomy and he is from Antakia.

١٣ الموصل

Of the famous Arabic fabrics (textile) that Europeans used throughout the Medieval Ages is the muslin or Al-Musilly in Arabic, it is a fabric that was made in the city of Mosel in Iraq.

١٤ دمشق

As for the famous Damascene, which was historically used for the clothes of the nobles and religious men, its name means the Damascene fabric in Arabic and it was made in the city of Damascus in Syria.

14·12

٦ عندما خسر اللعبة بكى ندماً.
بكى من الندم.
He cried out of regret.

٧ عندما شاهدت الفيلم سالت دموعها حزناً.
سالت دموعها من الحزن.
Her tears dropped out of sadness.

٨ عندما شرب الزجاجة وقع أرضاً.
وقع على الأرض.
He fell down on the floor.

٩ عندما ضربه الولد صاح ألماً.
صاح من الألم.
He screamed out of pain.

١٠ ابيض شعره شيباً عندما كبر في السن.
ابيض من الشيب.
His hair became white because of greying.

١ الغرفة باردة جدا نكاد نتجمد برداً.
نكاد نتجمد من البرد.
We are about to freeze because of the cold.

٢ لم يأكل شيئا منذ الصباح وهو يحس أنه يكاد يموت جوعاً.
يكاد يموت من الجوع.
He is about to die of hunger.

٣ عندما سمع النتيجة احمر غضباً.
احمر من الغضب.
He became red out of anger.

٤ عندما رأت الكلب اصفرت خوفاً.
اصفرت من الخوف.
She turned yellow out of fear.

٥ عندما سمع الخبر طار فرحاً.
طار من الفرح.
He jumped out of joy.

١ درست اللغة الفرنسية حباً بالشعر الفرنسي.
Out of love for French poetry
لحبها بالشعر الفرنسي

٢ جاء إلى لندن طلباً للدراسة.
In order to study
لطلب الدراسة

٣ سافر إلى دبي رغبة بالحصول على عمل.
Out of desire to get a job
لرغبته بالحصول على عمل

٤ لبست معطفها خوفاً من البرد.
Out of fear of cold
لخوفها من البرد

٥ انتظر أمام بيتها أملاً أن يراها.
Out of hope to see her
لأمله أن يراها

٦ غطت شعرها اتقاء للمطر.
Out of protection from the rain
لاتقاء المطر

٧ درس الطلاب استعداداً للامتحان.
To get ready for the exam
للاستعداد للامتحان.

٨ لن نمر من مركز المدينة تحاشياً للازدحام.
To avoid overcrowding
لتحاشي الازدحام

٩ درس الأدب الانكليزي عشقاً لشكسبير.
Out of fondness for Shakespeare
لعشقه لشكسبير

١٠ يعمل في التلفزيون سعياً وراء الشهرة.
In search of fame
لسعيه وراء الشهرة

١١ يحاولون التقرب منه طمعاً بأمواله.
Out of greed for his money
لطمعهم بأمواله

١٢ أفرغ كل خزاناته بحثاً عن الصورة الضائعة.
In search of the photo
بحثا عن الصورة

١ لبست ثوبا مخملياً من أجل الحفلة.
ثوباً من المخمل
A velvet dress

٢ أهداها عقداً ماسياً في عيد ميلادها.
عقداً من الماس
A diamond necklace

٣ اشترت قرطا فضياً من سوق الصناعات اليدوية.
قرطاً من الفضة
A silver earring

٤ هذا قميص قطني جيد للطقس الحار.
قميص من القطن
A cotton shirt

٥ وضعنا طعام الغداء في علبة بلاستيكية.
علبة من البلاستيك
A plastic box

٦ وضعوا الحلويات في كيس ورقي.
كيس من الورق
A paper bag

٧ سألبس كنزة صوفية لأن الطقس بارد.
كنزة من الصوف
A woolen pullover

٨ تلبس عباءة حريرية سوداء عندما تذهب إلى السعودية.
عباءة من الحرير
A silk gown

٩ وضعت في يدها سواراً ذهبياً.
سواراً من الذهب
A golden bracelet

١٠ سيحيطون حديقتهم بسور حديدي.
سور من الحديد
An iron fence

١١ أعطتها جدتها ملعقة نحاسية.
ملعقة من النحاس
A copper spoon

١٢ هو شخص قاس وله قلب حجري.
قلب من الحجر
A stone heart

١ ستحصل بسهولة على قبول في الجامعة بعد الحصول على المنحة.

من السهل الحصول على قبول في الجامعة بعد الحصول على المنحة.

It is easy to get admission in the university after obtaining a scholarship.

٢ الوصول إلى المسرح بدون سيارة صعب.

من الصعب الوصول إلى المسرح بدون سيارة.

It is difficult to reach the theater without a car.

٣ نتوقع وصول الوزير غداً.

من المتوقع أن يصل الوزير غداً.

It is expected that the minister will arrive tomorrow.

٤ قرر الرئيس أن يقوم بزيارة رسمية إلى أمريكا.

من المقرر أن يقوم الرئيس بزيارة رسمية إلى أمريكا.

It is decided (planned) that the president will make an official visit to America.

٥ يلزمنا أن نعود إلى البيت عند الغداء.

من اللازم أن نعود إلى البيت عند الغداء.

It is necessary to go home at lunch.

٦ إن عقد اجتماع هذا الشهر أمر محتمل.

من المحتمل عقد اجتماع هذا الشهر.

It is probable that a meeting will be held this month.

٧ حضور حفلة مع الأصدقاء القدامى أمر رائع.

من الرائع حضور حفلة مع الأصدقاء القدامى.

It is wonderful to attend a party with old friends.

٨ يمكننا أن نذهب إلى السينما يوم الجمعة.

من الممكن الذهاب إلى السينما يوم الجمعة.

It is possible to go to the cinema on Friday.

٩ غسل اليدين قبل تناول الطعام ضروري.

من الضروري غسل اليدين قبل تناول الطعام.

It is necessary to wash hands before having food.

١٠ يهمهم احترام زملاء العمل.

من المهم احترام زملاء العمل.

It is necessary to respect workmates.

15 Prepositions with interrogative and relative pronouns

٥ إلى أين يأخذكم هذا الشارع؟

Where does this street take you?

٦ إلام يلمح المحاضر؟

What is the lecturer hinting at?

٧ إلام تشير إشارة المرور هذه؟

What does this road sign point at?

٨ إلام/إلى من يلتفت الطفل؟

Who is the child turning to?

١ إلام ترمز الوردة الحمراء؟

What does the red rose symbolize?

٢ إلى أين يعود الغريب؟

Where will the stranger return to?

٣ إلام سيؤدي هذا النقاش؟

Where will this discussion lead to?

٤ إلام تنظر؟

What are you looking at?

I wrote the homework this evening with the new pen. ١

بم كتبت الوظيفة هذا المساء؟

The employees entertain themselves with computer games when they have a break in the office. ٢

بم يتسلى الموظفون عندما يكون لديهم استراحة في المكتب؟

I call my family and friends when I feel lonely. ٣

بمن تتصل عندما تشعر بالوحدة؟

The artist drew/has drawn the famous picture in black and white. ٤

بم رسم الفنان اللوحة الشهيرة؟

I seek help from my siblings when I face a problem. ٥

بمن تستعين حين تواجه في مشكلة؟

The director met the new employees today. ٦

بمن اجتمع المدير الجديد اليوم؟

My children play with their friends after school with the ball they bought last month. ٧

بم يلعب أطفالكِ مع أصدقائهم بعد المدرسة؟

People celebrate the coming of the New Year on the 31st of December. ٨

بم يحتفل الناس في الواحد والثلاثين من شهر كانون الثاني (ديسمبر)؟

I met my childhood friends when I traveled to my village last month. ٩

بمن التقيتَ/التقيتِ عندما سافرت إلى قريتك الشهر الماضي؟

I clean my hands with water and soap. ١٠

بم تنظف يديكَ بعد تناول الطعام؟

٥ علام تجيب هذه الجملة؟   ١ علام اتفق الفريقان؟

٦ علام يفاوضون؟   ٢ علام يبكي هذا الطفل؟

٧ علام تعتمد في تقييمكَ للطلاب؟   ٣ علام يتنافسون؟

٤ علام يدل هذا التصرف؟

The mother took the cat away from the child. ١

عمن أبعدت الأم القطة؟

You should put the child far from the stove. ٢

عم يجب إبعاد الطفل؟

I will ask about all my childhood friends when I visit my birthplace. ٣

عن أي من أصدقاء طفولتك ستسأل عندما تزور مسقط رأسك؟

The journalist will write the article about Najib Mahfouz. ٤

عمن سيكتب الصحفي المقالة؟

I asked the man on the street about the train station. ٥

عم سألت الرجل في الطريق؟

The lecturer talked about Arab–European relations. ٦

عم تكلم المحاضر؟

The police released some political detainees today. ٧

عمن أفرجت الشرطة اليوم؟

They are searching for solutions to the their problems. ٨

عم يبحثون؟

The teacher will talk about Sa'd allah Wannus in his lecture about Arab theater. ٩

عمن من المسرحيين العرب سيتحدث الأستاذ في درسه عن المسرح العربي؟

I resemble my parents but I differ from my father in respect to shape. ١٠

من تشبهين من والديك وعمن تختلفين أكثر؟

He defends his right to return to his country. ١١

عم يدافع؟

This poem expresses the poet's love for nature. ١٢

عم تعبر هذه القصيدة؟

15·5

٥ فيم ستشاركون خلال المهرجان؟   ١ فيم تفكر طوال الوقت؟

٦ فيمن تفكر؟   ٢ فيم ستضع كل هذه الكتب؟

٧ فيم ستجري بحثك القادم؟   ٣ فيم تورطوا؟

٤ فيمن تضع ثقتك؟

15·6

٦ لِمَ لم تتصل بنا اليوم؟   ١ لمن هذه السيارة؟

٧ لمن تلوحين بيدك؟   ٢ لِم انتقلت من بيتك القديم الجميل؟

٨ لِم أنت حزين؟   ٣ لمن ستعطي كتبك القديمة؟

٩ لِم تلبس كل هذه الثياب؟   ٤ لمن سترسل كل هذه البطاقات البريدية؟

١٠ لمن يبيع هذا الولد المجوهرات التقليدية؟   ٥ لِم/لماذا تمشي بسرعة؟

15·7

٥ ممن ستطلب المساعدة إذا وقعت في مشكلة؟   ١ ممن استعرت هذا القلم؟

٦ مم صنعت هذه الكعكة اللذيذة؟   ٢ ممن تأخذ مصروفك الشهري عادة؟

٧ مم تخاف عندما تمشي في الغابة؟   ٣ مم صنع هذا العقد الجميل؟

٨ ممن تلقيت هذه الرسالة؟   ٤ هو يغير بيته كثيراً، ممن يريد الهروب؟

15·8

١ صنعت كعكة عيد ميلادها مما اشترته من السوق.

She made the cake for her birthday with what she bought from the market.

مم صنعت كعكة عيد ميلادها؟

٢ استعدت الكتاب ممن استعاره مني.

I got my book back from the person who borrowed it.

ممن استعدتِ الكتاب؟

٣ سأنصح أطفالي بما نصحني به أبي.

I will advise my children about the things that my father advised me about.

بم ستنصح أطفالك حين يكبرون؟

٤ أخبرهم عما ينوي فعله.

He told them about what he intended to do.

ماذا أخبرهم؟

٥ أنا مستغرب مما قالوه.

I am astonished at what they have said.

مم أنت مستغرب؟

٦ معي من النقود أكثر مما معك.

I have more money than what you have.

كم معكَ من النقود؟

٧ عندما يقع خلاف بين أصدقائي أدافع دوما عمن يحتاجني أكثر.

When my friends have a disagreement I defend the one who needs me most.

عمن تدافع عندما يقع خلاف بين أصدقائك؟

٨ أفكر فيما قلته الآن.

I am thinking about what you have said now.

فيم تفكر؟

٩ حدثناهم عما فعلنا البارحة.

We told them about what we did yesterday.

عم حدثتموهم؟

١٠ يضع أمله فيمن يحبه من أهله أصدقائه.

He puts his hope in those he loves among his family and friends.

فيمن يضع أمله؟

١١ نعم، تعلم اللغة اللاتينية أصعب مما كنت أظن.

Learning the Latin language is more difficult than I thought.

هل كنت تظن أن تعلم اللغة اللاتينية صعب؟

١٢ شاهدوا فيلم رعب في التلفاز وهم خائفون مما مما شاهدوه.

They saw a horror movie on TV and they are scared of what they saw.

مم خافوا؟

١٣ أثق بمن يثق بي.

I trust those who trust me.

بمن تثق؟

١٤ غضب جارنا مما قلناه له.

Our neighbor got angry with what we have said to him.

لم غضب جاركم حين تكلمتم معه؟

١٥ أعط الكتب لمن يحتاجها.

Give the books to whoever needs them.

لمن يجب أن أعطي كتبي القديمة؟

١٦ عند عودتي سأسأل عمن سأل عني.

Upon my return I will ask about whoever asked about me.

عمن ستسأل عند عودتك؟

١٧ صديقي المريض يشكو <u>مما</u> يشكو منه والده.

My sick friend is suffering from the same illness as his father.

مم يشكو صديقك المريض؟

١٨ لم يستجب المدير <u>لما</u> طلبه الموظفون.

The director did not respond to what the employees requested.

هل استجاب المدير لطلبات الموظفين؟

١٩ لا، فدراسة اللغات أصعب <u>مما</u> توقعت.

Studying languages is more difficult than I had expected.

هل كنت تتوقع أن دراسة اللغات صعبة إلى هذا الحد؟

٢٠ استمتعنا <u>بما</u> قدموه من رقصات وما عزفوه من موسيقى.

We enjoyed the dances they performed and the music they played.

ما الذي استمتعتم به خلال السهرة؟

16 Practicing prepositions in context

16·1

١. My name is John.

٢. And I am from New York City.

٣. I study Arabic language at the Languages Institute at the University of Damascus.

٤. I live with George and he is a student from Britain.

٥. I moved into my new room a week ago.

٦. The room is located in a big house at the center of the old city behind the Umayyad mosque.

٧. At the center of the house there is a small garden in which there is a pond and a water fountain around which we have coffee in the morning and stay up late at night.

٨. To the right of the pond there is a jasmine tree and to the left there is a lemon tree.

٩. In front of the house there is a popular café where I meet my friends.

١٠. And next to that, there is a small restaurant. There are also several stores for selling antiques around it.

16·2

اسمي جون وأنا <u>من</u> مدينة نيويورك. أدرس اللغة العربية <u>في</u> معهد اللغات <u>في</u> جامعة دمشق. أسكن <u>مع</u> جورج وهو طالب <u>من</u> بريطانيا. انتقلت منذ أسبوع <u>إلى</u> غرفتي الجديدة. تقع الغرفة <u>في</u> بيت كبير وسط المدينة القديمة خلف الجامع الأموي. <u>في</u> وسط البيت حديقة صغيرة <u>فيها</u> بركة ونافورة ماء نشرب قربها القهوة <u>في</u> الصباح، ونسهر حولها <u>في</u> الليل. <u>على</u> يمين البركة شجرة ياسمين وعلى <u>يسارها</u> شجرة ليمون. <u>أمام البيت</u> مقهى شعبي ألتقي <u>فيه</u> مع أصدقائي، وقربه مطعم صغير، وهناك عدة محلات <u>لبيع</u> التحف حوله.

16·3

١ <u>من مدينة</u> single particle-preposition

٢ <u>في معهد</u> single particle-preposition

٣ <u>في جامعة</u> single particle-preposition

٤ <u>مع جورج</u> single particle-preposition

٥ <u>من بريطانيا</u> single particle-preposition

٦ <u>إلى غرفتي</u> single particle-preposition

٧ <u>في بيت</u> single particle-preposition

٨ <u>في وسط</u> compound preposition followed by **dharf** (*adverb of place*)

٩ <u>فيها</u> compound particle-preposition combined with an attached pronoun

١٠ في <u>الصباح</u> single particle-preposition

١١ في <u>الليل</u> single particle-preposition

١٢ <u>على</u> يمين compound particle-preposition combined with **dharf** (*adverb of place*)

١٣ <u>على</u> يسارها compound particle-preposition combined with **dharf** (*adverb of place*)

١٤ <u>فيه</u> compound particle-prepositrion combined with an attached pronoun

١٥ مع <u>أصدقائي</u> single particle-preposition

١٦ <u>لبيع</u> single particle-preposition

16·4
اتصل <u>بي</u> اليوم صديقي أيمن الذي يدرس <u>معي</u> <u>في</u> المدرسة الابتدائية وقال: "تبدو سعيداً جداً، <u>لماذا</u>؟"

قلت له "<u>لأننا</u> مسافرون."

قال: "<u>إلى أين</u>؟"

قلت له "أنا الآن مشغول. سأكتب <u>لك</u> رسالة إلكترونية بعد قليل."

قال: "ومتى ستعودون؟"

قلت: "لا أعرف." بعد دقائق كتبت <u>له</u> هذه الرسالة، وأرسلتها <u>بالبريد</u> الإلكتروني:

"أنا سعيد جداً هذا الصباح. بدأت اليوم عطلة أبي الصيفية. ستسافر عائلتي <u>إلى</u> مدينة طرطوس غداً <u>لقضاء</u> أسبوعين <u>في</u> المدينة وعلى شاطئها كما نفعل كل سنة. خرج أبي باكراً ليحجز تذاكر سفرنا. وضعت أمي <u>في</u> حقيبتنا الكبيرة ملابسي وملابس أخوتي الصيفية، وثياب سباحتنا وألعابنا المائية و آلات تصويرنا <u>بالإضافة إلى</u> كل ما اشتراه أبي <u>للعطلة</u>. طرطوس مدينة فينيقية جميلة، واسمها الفينيقي "أرادوس". البحر في تلك المدينة جميل، وأمواجه زرقاء.

أنا وأخوتي ووالدي نقضي يومنا عادة <u>في</u> السباحة <u>في</u> البحر، وبناء بيوت <u>على</u> رمله، بينما تشرب أمي قهوتها وهي تنظر <u>إلينا</u> من تحت المظلة.

كلنا نحب السمك، <u>ولذلك</u> نقضي وقت الغداء <u>في</u> المطاعم الجبلية، أو <u>في</u> جزيرة أرواد حيث نتناوله ونحن نستمتع <u>بالطبيعة</u> هناك.

<u>في</u> المساء ننزل <u>إلى</u> المدينة ونتمشى <u>في</u> شوارعها أو نزور أقاربنا وكل من يدعونا <u>من</u> أصدقاء والدي. ونخرج <u>معهم</u> أحيانا <u>إلى</u> المطاعم والمقاهي".

16·5
١ <u>بي</u> inseparable preposition, combined with an attachable pronoun

٢ <u>معي</u> separate preposition, combined with an attachable pronoun

٣ <u>في</u> separate preposition

٤ <u>لماذا</u> inseparable preposition, combined with interrogative article

٥ <u>له</u> inseparable prepositrion, combined with an attachable pronoun

٦ <u>لأننا</u> inseparable preposition combined with أنّ and an attachable prounoun

٧ <u>إلى أين</u> a preposition followed by an interrogative article

٨ <u>له</u> inseparable preposition, combined with an attachable pronoun

٩ <u>لك</u> inseparable preposition, combined with an attachable pronoun

١٠ <u>له</u> inseparable preposition, combined with an attachable pronoun

١١ <u>بالبريد</u> inseparable/attached preposition

١٢ <u>إلى</u> separate preposition

١٣ <u>لقضاء</u> inseparable/attached preposition

separate preposition في ١٤

separate preposition على ١٥

separate preposition في ١٦

inseparable preposition بالإضافة ١٧

separate preposition إلى ١٨

inseparable preposition للعطلة ١٩

separate preposition في ٢٠

separate preposition في ٢١

separate preposition على ٢٢

preposition attached to a pronoun إلينا ٢٣

separate preposition followed by **dharf makan** (*adverb of place*) من تحت ٢٤

inseparable preposition combined with a demonstrative pronoun لذلك ٢٥

separate preposition في ٢٦

separate preposition في ٢٧

inseparable preposition بالطبيعة ٢٨

separate preposition في ٢٩

separate preposition إلى ٣٠

separate preposition في ٣١

separate preposition من ٣٢

preposition attached to a pronoun معهم ٣٣

separate preposition إلى ٣٤

16·6 My friend Ayman, who studies with me in the elementary school, called me today and said, "You seem happy, why?"

I said, "Because we are going on vacation."

He said, "Where?"

I said, "I am busy right now. I will write an e-mail to you in a short while."

He said, "And when are you coming back?"

I said, "I don't know." A few minutes later, I wrote the following letter and I sent it to him by e-mail:

"I am very happy this morning. My father's vacation started today. My family will travel to Tartous tomorrow to spend two weeks in the city and on its beach as we do every summer. My father has left early to book our travel tickets. In our big suitcase my mother has packed my clothes and the clothes of my siblings, our swimming suits, our water toys, and our camera in addition to whatever my father had bought for the holiday.

Tartous is a beautiful Phoenician city. Its Phoenician name is 'Aradous.' The sea in this city is beautiful and its waves are blue. My brothers, father, and I usually spend our day swimming in the sea and building houses on the sand, while my mom drinks her coffee and watches us from under the umbrella.

We all love fish and that is why we spend our lunch time at the restaurants in the mountains or on the island of Arwad enjoying nature while having lunch.

In the evening, we go down to the city and walk on its streets or we visit our relatives or whoever of my father's friends invites us. Sometimes we go to restaurants and cafés with them."